"This is God's time for men! He is graciously stirring in our hearts and sounding the clear call to godliness. *Guard Your Heart* deals with the 'above all else' issues in our lives, exposing deadly snares and providing steps toward safety and protection."

STEVE GREEN
Recording Artist

"Gary Rosberg is a leader calling forth a spiritual awakening in the hearts of men. *Guard Your Heart* speaks directly to the men of today. We are challenged to make a clear commitment to faith in Jesus Christ, to being a loving and devoted husband and father, to spiritual leadership in our family, and to being there to help and encourage our friends and the larger community. This is a powerful message and is helping stir a movement across America."

TERRY E. BRANSTAD
Governor of Iowa

"Gary Rosberg brings hope and perspective for men who want to win in life. Chapter Eight on sexual temptations is worth the price of the book and is must reading for every man."

DENNIS RAINEY
Executive Director, FamilyLife
and co-author of BUILDING YOUR MATE'S SELF-ESTEEM

"Millions of men are trying to guard their physical hearts. Few have the wisdom to guard their spiritual hearts. I highly recommend *Guard Your Heart*—it could save you a very painful triple by-pass later on."

STEVE FARRAR
President, Men's Leadership, Dallas
and author of POINT MAN

"In *Guard Your Heart* Dr. Gary Rosberg provides simple yet significant steps men can take to be and become more than conquerors. His valuable insights for dealing with sexual temptation and overcoming passivity are especially powerful. With the conviction of a man who knows the Word of God and the practicality of a man who has been on the front lines facing hard issues, Gary gives men the tools they need to go beyond inspiration and insight to practical application."

GARY J. OLIVER, Ph.D.
Associate Professor, Denver Seminary
and author of REAL MEN HAVE FEELINGS TOO

"In the war zone that faces each of us as Christian men today, I can't think of a better book to read alongside your Bible than this one you're holding. *Guard Your Heart* is the book I'm taking the men in my Bible study through, and one I'm reading myself. It's an honest, well-written, challenging message to stay in the battle and fight the good fight. Even better, it's written by a man I know well who loves God and his family, and who I respect as one of this nation's leading spokesmen for the family."

JOHN TRENT
co-author of THE BLESSING

"Gary Rosberg is a good man and a great friend. With 20,000 hours of counseling men and women under his professional belt, he's well qualified to coach men in the things that matter most. The chapter on passivity is especially striking. Tracing man's slide from the saddle to the couch, Gary calls every man to wake up and get a grip on the reins of his heart."

STU WEBER
Pastor, Good Shepherd Community Church in Boring, Oregon
and author of TENDER WARRIOR

GUARD YOUR HEART

GUARD YOUR HEART

FOR OUT OF IT
WILL FLOW YOUR
LIFE STORY

■

DR. GARY ROSBERG

MULTNOMAH BOOKS

If you would like to inquire about Dr. Gary Rosberg conducting a couple's conference, men's conference,
corporate meeting, or church seminar in your community, please contact him at:

CrossTrainer Ministries

1200 35th Street, Suite 507

West Des Moines, Iowa 50266

(515) 225-8009

Please note: All names of clients and details of their lives have been altered,
combined with other cases, and fictionalized in order to protect the privacy of their identities.
Any resemblance to any particular person is unintended.

Unless otherwise indicated, all Scripture references are from the
New International Version, © 1973, 1978, 1984 by International Bible Society.
Used by permission of Zondervan Publishing House. All rights reserved.
The "NIV" and "New International Version" trademarks are registered
in the United States Patent and Trademark Office by International Bible Society.
Use of either trademark requires the permission of International Bible Society.
Scripture references marked TLB are from *The Living Bible,* © 1971 by Tyndale House Publishers,
Wheaton, Illinois. Used by permission.
The anecdotes at the beginning of Chapter 9 are from *Great American Anecdotes,*
John and Claire Whitcomb (New York: William Morrow and Company, 1993).

94 95 96 97 98 99 00 01 02 03 — 10 9 8 7 6 5 4 3 2 1

Guard your heart
Guard your heart
Don't trade it for treasure
Don't give it away
Guard your heart
Guard your heart
As a payment for pleasure
It's a high price to pay
For a soul that remains sincere
With a conscience clear—
Guard your heart

lyrics & music by JON MOHR
©1989 Birdwing Music (ASCAP)
Used by permission

CONTENTS

INTRODUCTION Let's Be Careful Out There *15*

CHAPTER ONE Out of the Fog *21*

CHAPTER TWO How Will I Be Remembered? *31*

CHAPTER THREE What It Means to Guard Your Heart *45*

CHAPTER FOUR Castles Under Fire *57*

CHAPTER FIVE Frontal Attack #1: Career Pressures *71*

CHAPTER SIX Frontal Attack #2: Distractions *89*

CHAPTER SEVEN Frontal Attack #3: Relationship Pressures *99*

CHAPTER EIGHT Frontal Attack #4: Sexual Temptation *117*

CHAPTER NINE Sneak Attack #1: The Search for Significance *133*

CHAPTER TEN Sneak Attack #2: Passivity *145*

CHAPTER ELEVEN Sneak Attack #3: Control *159*

CHAPTER TWELVE Sneak Attack #4: Competition *173*

CHAPTER THIRTEEN Christianity Is a Team Sport *189*

CHAPTER FOURTEEN Three Rocks *201*

CONCLUSION Guarding Your Life Story *211*

FOR WOMEN ONLY

A special section by Barbara Rosberg:
Helping Your Husband Guard His Heart *219*

ACKNOWLEDGMENTS

A funny thing happened to me on the way to the summer floods of 1993.

I was sitting in my hotel room in Atlanta, preparing for the first day of the Christian Booksellers Convention. Along with all of America, I turned on CNN and watched scenes of people throughout our fine country laboring night and day to save life and livelihood from the raging waters of our Midwestern rivers.

That's when it hit home. For on that very day, the river in my hometown of West Des Moines, Iowa, leaped over its banks and shut down the city's water supply. Calling home from my hotel room, I learned that my wife and two daughters were helping to sandbag the river.

I didn't need to be in Atlanta right then. I needed to be home.

A week scheduled full of interviews, dinners, meetings, and networking, had to be tossed aside. Immediately. I had just two hours to hit the convention floor to excuse myself from my commitments. On my way out the door of the convention, somewhat rattled not knowing what I was going to face at home, I knew I was forgetting something. I vaguely recalled a promise I had made to my best friend, Steve Farrar.

The promise? To stop and introduce myself to a guy named Don Jacobson, publisher and president of Questar Publishers, in Sisters, Oregon.

So, glancing at my watch, I raced back to Questar's booth and caught Don. After a brief introduction, we took my remaining thirty minutes to get acquainted. And my life has not been quite the same since then. I knew he was my kind of man: a man sold out to his family and to Jesus Christ. He also was on a mission in life. You know the kind of guy. You meet them rarely but when you do, you know they are different. Don's mission was simple: to bring honor to God by publishing quality books and resources for His people. And he wasn't alone in his commitment. He had surrounded himself

10

with a group of men and women in Central Oregon and had committed his "team of partners" to put out the best of the best for the glory of Jesus Christ. It was a match. Don, thanks for the brief encounter of the wildest kind on a couple of folding chairs in Atlanta.

So it is with this acknowledgment that I recognize many of the people who have made *Guard Your Heart* a reality. First of all to Don and Brenda Jacobson and the Questar family. You are golden. Thanks for making me feel at home. From gracious Cheryl Reinertson at "command central" to Blake Weber, the best assistant to a publisher in the history of mankind. You two are the best.

Dan and Scharlotte Rich, your teamwork in marriage is an honor to watch. Dan, no one and I mean no one, has the mixture of talent and obedience that you have in bringing quality works to the hearts and homes of our country and world. Thanks for your obedience.

Steve Cobb, Eric Weber, and Doug Gabbert, you all round out a team that has been called by the Father to do great things. Stay faithful my friends.

To the editorial crew at Questar. I know several hands and several sets of eyes went through these pages. When the pressure was on, you guys came through. I'm grateful to you all. Steve Halliday, Thomas Womack, and Shari MacDonald deserve kudos for their investment in this manuscript. I want to honor most of all my editor, Larry Libby. You are a truly gifted wordsmith. But more importantly, you are my friend. You exceeded our greatest expectations, Larry. This book was meant to be, and you were meant to help me craft it up front, shape it during its awkward growth stages, and bring it home in the ninth inning. Barbara and I honor you and love you, Larry. Get some rest.

There are a few men that surround me that also need to know my heart. Steve Farrar more than any other. Thanks for being more than a friend to hang out with…you're my brother. Together, we dream about healthy homes throughout our land, stretch each other to the brink, and know that

God has life-changing plans ahead. Continue to stand tall. I pray we finish the race well, Steve. Together. Guard your heart.

To John Trent. You were there when my first book was a dream and you challenged me to make it happen. It did, but not without you. You encouraged me on with this one. You and Cindy are loved by the Rosbergs, good friend. Thanks for the privilege of being your pal.

To Stu Weber, the ultimate tender warrior. What a great title and representation of who you are. God has brought the streams of our lives together. I am honored to go down the stream with you, amigo.

And now a little closer to the homefront, my accountability team. Jerry Foster, Tim Vermillion, and Mike Colby. After fifteen years of weekly meetings, I still look forward to them with great hope and anticipation. You helped me to win in my family when I thought I could never lead it again. You have remained faithful. Thanks for your friendship. See you Tuesday.

Tom Evans, you round out my local group of guys with Magdi Ghali and Duane Tolander on my board. I need all three of you. Thanks for sticking close to the Savior. Your direction is godly and needed.

To the men of CrossTrainer Ministries. You have been my plumb line as I have written these pages. As of today there are over 450 of you in Des Moines and hundreds more across the country. You amaze me with your willingness to roll out of the sheets each Wednesday morning. I am committed to leading you well and guarding my own heart. Thanks for the privilege of teaching you each Wednesday. I promise to stay obedient. Let me know if you see a drift.

To my hometown team at the office of Family Legacy. What a great group. To Tom VanderWell, my right hand, thanks for being there day in and day out. You have freed me up to do what God has called me to. You are a faithful man, Tom. To Tanya Wozniuk, my left hand, you are a Godsend. He has great plans for you. To Cindy Berg and Donna Van Persuem up at command central. You do it so well. To our counselors: Don

Gilbert, Randy Kiel, Ed and Pat Ashby, Deb Gipple, and John Steddom. Thousands of families have been ministered to because of your faithfulness. Stay obedient.

I am thankful to Pastor Linton Lundeen and his teaming up with me in the research of the Proverbs. Also to Pastor Quintin Steiff for his weekly dividing of the Word which is such regular encouragement. To Bob and Lois Vermeer: You have been more instrumental in freeing me up to do what God has called me to than you will ever know. Thanks for helping to equip me. You are making a difference.

And now to the best part.

Mom and Dad. You two are terrific. Dad, you taught me to be a man, to honor others, and to love my wife and my country. Mom, you taught me to be tender, yet wise. Thanks for just being who you are. Talk to you Tuesday afternoon, Mom. I promise.

To Sarah and Missy. You give me the honor of calling you my girls. I am proud of you both. You are my favorite people in the whole world. God has brought you both into "teendom" with poise, courage, and hearts sold out to Jesus Christ. Stay faithful to Him, girls. He loves you, yes, even more than your mom and I do.

And to Barbara, my friend, my hero, my partner. You got this whole thing going, Barb. Remember back in college when you said, "Gary, unless you know Jesus Christ, there isn't any future for us"? You blew me away. As a new Christian you took a stand that sent me into a five month search for the Truth. And I found Him. Thanks for staying obedient. You have remained faithful to me and I to you. I honor you above all others in this world. I promise to finish the race as a "knight of one lady." Our castle is safe. You are my one and only lady, Barbara. I love you.

....

"LET'S BE CAREFUL OUT THERE..."

■

One thing—and probably only one—remained constant in the organized chaos that was Hill Street Precinct.

As the morning muster wrapped up and the gathered police officers reached for their gear to hit the chancy streets, Sergeant Phil Esterhaus would put down his sheaf of papers, look out across his charges in the squad room, and utter the same five-word caution:

"Let's be careful out there."

The uniformed troops would linger a moment as if waiting for those very words, then file out of the room and fan across the city.

Sgt. Esterhaus knew his officers were headed into unpredictable crises and dangers. They could get caught in a crossfire. They could get jumped in an alley. They could be drawn into a compromising situation. They could be assaulted while writing out a routine traffic violation. Anything could happen on the hard-hitting 1980s television drama "Hill Street Blues."

As you may remember, each episode started with Esterhaus summoning the officers for roll call. Detective LaRue would be clowning around, Lieutenant

Howard Hunter would be readying his SWAT team, and Captain Frank Furillo would be anticipating the course of the day in the urban ghetto.

Just about every kind of crisis a creative script writer could imagine visited that precinct during its half dozen years on prime time. That's why the sergeant's parting benediction to his blue knights always seemed so fitting.

"Let's be careful out there."

That's a good word for cops cruising mean streets and unpredictable beats in a big city. It's also a good word for men like you and me heading out the front door every day to face our own battery of threats and dangers and challenges.

Let's be careful out there.

It worked for Hill Street's finest, and it works for each of us men today. You may feel as if you face your own set of crises each morning…

How I will I pay all the bills due by the end of the month?

Will I have a job by the end of the month?

Will my wife turn back to me—even though I've almost lost her?

Will that redhead get transferred so I can concentrate on work and not temptation?

Can I get back into my kids' lives after checking out for too long?

Your dilemmas may be there in the list above, or you may keep a short list of your own. But one thing remains true for guys like you and me. We need to be careful out there. We need to be wide awake. We need to be ready for the inevitable spiritual attacks, whether they're subtle and sneaky or full-blown frontal assaults.

God's Word, God's Warning

You don't have to take my word for it. Jesus said it again and again: "Be on your guard." Be on your guard, He said, against hypocrisy (Matthew 16:6-12), against greed (Luke 12:15), against persecution from others (Matthew 10:17), against false teaching (Mark 13:22-23), and above all, against spiritual slackness and unreadiness for the Lord's return (Mark 13:32-37). "Be careful," He said in Luke 21:34, "or your hearts will be weighed down with dissipation [*another word for wild living],* drunkenness, and the anxieties of life *[wildness may not be your problem, but maybe worry is]."*

The same caution echoes throughout the Scriptures. Listen, and let each warning have its due: *"Be careful* that you don't fall" (1 Corinthians 10:12). *"Be careful* to do what is right" (Romans 12:17). *"Be very careful,* then, how you live" (Ephesians 5:15). *"Be careful* that none of you be found to have fallen short" (Hebrews 4:1). *"Only be careful,* and watch yourselves" (Deuteronomy 4:9). *"Be careful* to do what the Lord your God has commanded you" (Deuteronomy 5:32). *"Be careful* that you do not forget the Lord" (Deuteronomy 6:12). *"Be careful* to obey all that is written in the Book" (Joshua 23:6). "I am the Lord your God…*be careful* to keep my laws" (Ezekiel 20:19). *"Give careful thought* to your ways" (Haggai 1:5-7).

Be careful. Watch out. Be on guard. Because if we don't get hit today, you can bet we will tomorrow or the day after. It's that kind of world out there, and it doesn't take a Hollywood writer to script the kind of hazards and dangers facing a family man in America.

That's why we need the Lord. That's why we need our families. And that's why we need each other. We need other men to watch our backs, to monitor our blind spots, to hang in with us over the long haul.

When LaRue and Washington hit the alleys and avenues of Hill Street Precinct, they were on the lookout for each other. Detective Harry Goldblume covered for Lucy back at the chaotic station and Lt. Hunter was always looking for an opportunity to call out the SWAT team to "get the streets under control."

Let me ask you: Which streets in your life are out of control—or getting close to it?

Where is the enemy lurking in your precinct?

From which rooftop is he sniping at your back?

Just like the officers of Hill Street, we men need to be alert. Alert for the enemy. Sometimes he's hanging out in dark alleyways. Sometimes he'll step out from behind a building and take us on face to face.

Whichever way he comes, he always goes for the heart. That's why we need to guard our hearts. Because just when we begin to relax that guard, he swoops in and nails us.

This isn't the kind of enemy you want to go one-on-one with. When the crunch comes, you want some guys watching your unprotected flank—guys you can trust your life with.

Paul must have been thinking about that type of friendship when he penned a few words to his young buddy Timothy. The old missionary soldier wrote: "I have fought the good fight. I have finished the race, I have kept the faith" (1 Timothy 4:7). When you're nearing the end of your life, wouldn't you love to send a letter to a close friend and boldly say words like that? *It's been a bloody fight, but I've hung in there to the last round. It's been a tough race, but I'm going to cross the tape. It's been a constant battle to hang on to my faith and integrity through it all, but here I am, still in one piece, ready to face my Lord.*

Paul rode solo at times in his ministry, but when things were quiet he also reflected on the friendships that sustained him at vulnerable moments. Timothy was Paul's friend through up and down, hot and cold, fat and lean. Who are your friends? And who calls you "friend"? If the answer to those two questions is a little hazy, stay with me awhile. Keep reading.

I don't know about you, but I wouldn't want to ride solo in a squad car through the mean streets of some of America's concrete jungles. That would be stupid. I believe it's even more stupid to ride solo through life as a man in a man-killing culture.

So I don't.

Do you?

Here's the punch line: If you're alone in this thing called the Christian walk, if you're trying to lead your family as some kind of maverick—a lone bull out ahead of the herd, walking straight into the storm—you're setting yourself up for a fall. You aren't Rambo or Robocop. And neither am I. Just like urban cops need their partners on the street, you and I need partners too. It doesn't matter if we spend our time in the boardroom or on the assembly line or in the governor's mansion. If you're anything like me, you've admitted your need to let some other men into your life to ask you the hard questions. Men who aren't impressed with you. Men who care enough about you to get in your face when you need it, and sometimes when you don't—just to keep you on your toes.

I have some men in my life who do that with me.

It isn't always convenient, it isn't always comfortable, but man, do I need them.

Why Listen to Me?

Why do I have anything to tell you about men and families in crisis? Is it because of my degree in counseling? That degree has helped arm me with a lot of ammo in learning to understand men and women, but it isn't my greatest qualification. My number one qualification for taking a stand on this one is that *I've been there.*

In 1983 I was staring at the frightening potential of losing my own family. Late one night, with the lights out, I asked my wife the scariest question of my life.

"Barb, can I come home?"

No, I wasn't gone physically, I wasn't living away from home. And no, I hadn't tossed it over spiritually through some gross sin or immorality. My body and spirit were still at home, but my attention and focus had been somewhere else for a long time—longer than I wanted to admit. I had sold out to my career. I was winning in the marketplace, but losing at home.

"Barb," I whispered into the darkness, "can I return and be the leader of this family God designed me to be? I want to be your husband again. I want to be a father to my daughters."

Gracious encourager that she is, Barbara said yes. And that was the beginning of my journey home. Home to the place where I was needed more than my career or culture would ever need me.

I am home now. In fact, I've been back for ten years, and I'm not leaving again. It wasn't a quick return, and it wasn't easy. It took time: time with my wife, time with my kids, time with my calendar. And time with my Lord. It took sweat, effort, and sacrifice to rebuild my family and my role as the leader of my home. But I am home. And I have learned from working with thousands of men and their families some keys to help guys guard their hearts.

I don't think there has ever been a better time in the history of our country to be men than today. But we need a battle plan. We need endurance and guts to finish the race. And we need a friend or two to run with us and help us dodge the swamps, low-lying roots, and half-hidden rocks that would bog us down or trip us up.

Sergeant Esterhaus said it well: "Let's be careful out there."

King Solomon said it even better: "Guard your heart."

....

CHAPTER ONE

Out of the Fog

■

I was sitting in my favorite chair, studying for the final stages of my doctoral degree, when Sarah announced herself in my presence with a question: "Daddy, do you want to see my family picture?"

"Sarah, Daddy's busy. Come back in a little while, Honey."

Good move, right? I *was* busy. A week's worth of work to squeeze into a weekend. You've been there.

Ten minutes later she swept back into the living room, "Daddy, let me show you my picture."

The heat went up around my collar. "Sarah, I said come back *later*. This is important."

Three minutes later she stormed into the living room, got three inches from my nose, and barked with all the power a five-year-old could muster: "Do you want to see it or don't you?" The assertive Christian woman in training.

"NO," I told her, "I DON'T."

With that she zoomed out of the room and left me alone. And somehow, being alone at that moment wasn't as satisfying as I thought it would be. I felt like a jerk. (Don't agree so loudly.) I went to the front door.

"Sarah," I called, "could you come back inside a minute, please? Daddy would like to see your picture."

She obliged with no recriminations, and popped up on my lap.

It was a great picture. She'd even given it a title. Across the top, in her best printing, she had inscribed: "OUR FAMILY BEST."

"Tell me about it," I said.

"Here is Mommy [a stick figure with long yellow curly hair], here is me standing by Mommy [with a smiley face], here is our dog Katie, and here is Missy [her little sister was a stick figure lying in the street in front of the house, about three times bigger than anyone else]. It was a pretty good insight into how she saw our family.

"I love your picture, Honey," I told her. "I'll hang it on the dining room wall, and each night when I come home from work and from class [which was usually around 10 P.M.], I'm going to look at it."

She took me at my word, beamed ear to ear, and went outside to play. I went back to my books. But for some reason I kept reading the same paragraph over and over.

Something was making me uneasy.

Something about Sarah's picture.

Something was missing.

I went to the front door. "Sarah," I called, "could you come back inside a minute, please? I want to look at your picture again, Honey."

Sarah crawled back into my lap. I can close my eyes right now and see the way she looked. Cheeks rosy from playing outside. Pigtails. Strawberry Shortcake tennis shoes. A Cabbage Patch doll named Nellie tucked limply under her arm.

I asked my little girl a question, but I wasn't sure I wanted to hear the answer.

"Honey...there's Mommy, and Sarah, and Missy. Katie the dog is in the picture, and the sun, and the house, and squirrels, and birdies. But Sarah...*where is your Daddy?*"

"You're at the library," she said.

With that simple statement my little princess stopped time for me. Lifting her gently off my lap, I sent her back to play in the spring sunshine. I slumped back in my chair with a swirling head and blood pumping furiously through my heart. Even as I type these words into the computer, I can feel those sensations all over again. It was a frightening moment. The fog lifted from my preoccupied brain for a moment—and suddenly I could see. But what I saw scared me to death. It was like being in a ship and coming out of the fog in time to see a huge, sharp rock knifing through the surf just off the port bow.

She nailed me. Right between the eyes. Bull's-eye. For whatever reason, I couldn't hear those words from Barbara, though she'd probably been trying to get through to me for months on end. All of the cautions to keep the "balanced lifestyle" from sermons, books, and friends never filtered through my distracted head. But Sarah's simple pronouncement—"You're at the library"—got my attention big time.

Plain, Unvarnished Truth

I hung the drawing on the dining room wall, just as I promised my girl. And through those long, intense weeks preceding the oral defense of my dissertation, I stared at that revealing portrait. It happened every night in the silence of my sleeping home, as I consumed my late-night, warmed-over dinners. I didn't have the guts to bring the issue up to Barbara. And she had the incredible insight to let it rest until I had the courage to deal with it.

I finally finished my degree program. I was "Dr. Rosberg" now, and I guess it should have been a big deal for me. But frankly, there wasn't much joy. It felt a little hollow. One night after graduation, Barbara and I were lying in bed together and I found myself working up the nerve to ask her a question. Actually there were three questions, progressively harder.

It was late, it was dark, and as I murmured my first question, I was praying Barb had already fallen asleep.

"Barb, are you sleeping?"

"No."

Rats! I thought to myself. *Now I'm committed.*

Question number two.

"Barbara, you've obviously seen Sarah's picture taped on the dining room wall. Why haven't you said anything?"

"Because I know how much it has wounded you, Gary."

Words from a wise woman, wise beyond her twenty-something years. At that point, I asked the tough question I mentioned a few pages back…the toughest question I've ever asked anyone in my entire life.

"Barb?"

"Yes, Gary?"

"Barb…I want to come home. Can I do it?"

Twenty seconds of silence followed. It seemed like I held my breath for an hour.

"Gary," Barb said carefully, "the girls and I love you very much. We want you home. But you haven't been here. I've felt like a single parent for years."

The words look cold in print, but she said them with restraint and tenderness. It was just plain, unvarnished truth. My little girl had drawn the picture, and now her mom was speaking the words. I lay there in the dark, pretending to sleep. But I couldn't. Events raced through my mind. I remembered when Missy was two and wouldn't sit on my lap for more than a few seconds. Why? Because she "didn't know her daddy." I recalled missed dinners with friends, evenings Barbara waited for me to come home but I had to study just a little longer, vacations canceled so I could finish a class. My life had been out of control, my family was on automatic pilot, and I had a long road ahead of me if I wanted to win them back.

But I *had* to win them back. Now that the fog had lifted, it suddenly became the most important thing in my life.

I tell this story for one reason. As you and I journey together through this book and learn to guard our hearts, I want you to know that I've been there. I've wrestled with the pain. I've lain in bed at night, my face wet with mingled sweat and tears. I've sat at the kitchen table with my little family and wondered how I was ever going to penetrate those hearts enough for them to trust me again. I know what it is to blow it in my leadership role—the role prescribed for men in Ephesians 5. I know what it is to sail around in an insensible fog, leaving my wife and daughters to fend for themselves out in the open sea without compass or captain.

I knew I needed to get back into that leader's post, but I couldn't demand it or announce it.

I had to *serve* my way back.

Over the coming months and years, it meant I had to sacrifice much of what I wanted to do for Gary in order to develop the trust from the three precious ladies in my life: Barbara and Sarah and Missy. You'll learn more about how I did that throughout this book.

Thank God, He allowed me to "come home." Thank God, He allowed me to see the need.

Big as a Mountain

Maybe you've been there. Something was right in front of you, big as a mountain, but you couldn't see it.

On my first trip to the Pacific Northwest, I flew into Seattle-Tacoma International in the dark, lucky to get in ahead of the fog. I saw nothing of the local scenery.

My hotel was right on Puget Sound, and as I checked in around midnight I could hear foghorns echoing over the water, taking me back to boyhood memories of Lake Michigan. But still I could see nothing out the window of my room.

Which was fine, really. All I wanted to see at that point was my pillow and the inside of my eyelids. The six o'clock wake-up call would come far too early. I snarfed down the little bag of airline peanuts I'd saved, hit the lights, and went comatose between the sheets.

It seemed like the phone rang five minutes later. The chipper voice on the line said, "Mr. Rosberg, good morning. It's 6:00 A.M."

No way, tell me it isn't morning.

I opened one eye and sure enough, the sun was peeping beneath a corner of the curtain. I threw my unwilling legs out of the covers and sat on the edge of the bed, listening again to the alluring sounds of water. Sea gulls. Surf. The muted wail of a distant ferry boat.

Drawn magnetically to the window, I pulled open the curtains. There was the water, all right, and something more. Something I hadn't seen—or even imagined—the night before.

Mount Rainier. Filling the horizon. Filling the window. Filling my unbelieving eyes. Gleaming white and purple and gold in the morning sunlight. Bigger than any mountain I'd ever seen.

I stood there a moment with my mouth open. "Unbelievable!" I said out loud. "Where did *that* come from?"

I have to admit I wasn't the greatest geography student in high school. (In fact, I wasn't the greatest student of anything in high school.) I knew Mount Rainier was "out there somewhere" in the Pacific Northwest. But not here, parked outside my hotel window.

That 14,000-foot hunk of rock didn't just "show up" during my brief six hours of slumber, however. It was there before I went to sleep. It had been there for millennia before I was born. It was there all the time I was growing up in the Midwest. Everyone in Seattle knew it was there.

But I didn't. And I couldn't see it—at least not until the darkness and the fog were gone and the curtains flung open. And then, there it was. Something in plain sight to everyone else came in plain sight to me. I could finally see.

Back in the Picture

Here's a question for you: Where's the fog in your life? Where's the darkness? Are there any curtains waiting to be opened wide?

Has a gray gloom drifted into the relationship with your wife? Has it chilled the closeness you want with your kids? Is there a damp darkness hiding your perspective of the great big God who loves you? Or maybe a clear view of Him and of your life is blocked by thick curtains drawn tightly before your eyes, curtains of busyness or preoccupation with things.

What will it take before we finally see?

Sometimes people near to us try to grab our attention. Our kids scream out until they realize we won't respond. So they get our attention some other way.

Our wives go from whispering, to shouting, to silence, sometimes concluding in their loneliness that the man they married is lost somewhere. Where and when did things change?

Our parents desire relationship with us in their latter years, but as their clock ticks down, ours winds up. We're just too busy.

Our Lord and Creator knows that we don't seek His presence like we used to. We're distracted, self-absorbed. We forget to look up at the Father who loves us. We forget to consider the Savior who died for us and the Holy Spirit who indwells us. God is right there, bigger than a mountain shining white and gold in the sunrise. We just can't see Him. We're in some kind of fog.

Fog is nothing new, either on mountains or in a man's head. It can keep a flatlander ignorant of a towering peak outside his window, and it can keep a busy man ignorant of critical situations right under his own nose. The bottom line is, sometimes that fog needs to get penetrated.

God has any number of means at His disposal to slice through the haze and mist and get our attention. Are you letting Him get yours?

After He got mine—with my daughter's devastating family portrait—it took a couple of years before I finally celebrated "being home." It was a banner day for me as the three most important people in my life announced they had a gift for me. I smiled widely...until five-year-old Missy said it was a "drawing of our family." I know this sounds crazy, but my heart started thudding hard in my chest. There it was again, the wide-lined sheet of tablet paper festooned with colorful crayon figures, this time drawn by our youngest. My eyes scanned the family representation. There was Barbara with the yellow hair. There was Sarah. And Missy. And Katie the dog. And a big sun smiling down out of the sky.

And there was a tall guy with a mustache, standing smack in the middle of his family.

Daddy.

I was back in the picture. Back where I belonged. It was time to go out to 31 Flavors and celebrate with some big-time, double-dip cholesterol busters.

Missy's complete family picture still hangs over my desk in my counseling office. Each day as I work with hurting families needing hope, I keep that little portrait in the corner of my eye. It's a little reminder that I want to be in the picture from now on. But just like you, I have to renew that commitment every time the sun comes up on a new day. It never gets easy, but the payoff is bigger than I could have dreamed.

Why You Can Win This Battle

You may be at the starting line right now, facing the biggest challenge of your life. You're coming out of the fog and seeing a few mountain-sized needs in your family circle. You're feeling out of sync as the leader of your home, and it hurts to think about opportunities you've missed. You're asking yourself, "Can I win this battle?"

God's answer is "Yes—with Me, you can." It doesn't matter where you are. God knows your heart and what to do about it. He knows if it's broken or hardened or out of tune. He knows your hidden strengths and your all-too-obvious weaknesses. "Even the very hairs of your head are all numbered" (Matthew 10:30).

He *knows* you. He knows exactly what you need, and He's there, twenty-four hours a day, to listen, respond, and give direction. Call on Him. You need Him. He's telling you to guard your heart, and He'll give you the will-power and the fire-power to do just that.

I'll leave you with one last, two-part question: What will be the *long-term* impact for your family if you recognize the fog, get your head above it, and set a fresh course with God? And what will be the *long-term* impact if you don't?

If you've begun to wrestle seriously with those words, my friend, you're already on your way.

Application Suggestions:

1. On a sheet of paper, write down one area in your life which you would say is most in danger of getting "out of control" (or perhaps it's already there).

2. What were your reasons for choosing this particular area of danger that you identified? On the same sheet of paper, make a few notes about the evidence that led to your choice.

3. Now review the list of Scriptural warnings given under the heading "God's Word, God's Warning" in the introduction to this book. Select one of these warnings which you believe pertains best to the danger area you indicated. Then write down the warning and its Scripture reference at the top of your sheet of paper.

4. Make a commitment to carry this sheet of paper with you for the next seven days. Use it to help you pray each morning and each evening for God's help in bringing and keeping under control this area of your life.

To Think About & Discuss:

1. Look at Philippians 4:7. According to this verse, what is it exactly that will guard our hearts and minds? And according to the previous verse (4:6), what do we need to do in order to experience it?

2. Look at the command about "waking up" in Ephesians 5:14, and think about it in light of the instructions for husbands in verses 25-31. In what ways might we as men seem "asleep" or "dead" when it comes to this area of loving leadership in the home? What is Christ's promise in verse 14 for those who do "wake up"?

3. Read the promise of Christ's return in 1 Thessalonians 5:5-8. How can these verses help us "wake up" to our roles as husbands and fathers?

....

CHAPTER TWO

HOW WILL I BE REMEMBERED?

■

My secretary stuck the slip of paper in my hand, and said, "Gary, don't forget your messages before you go into your next appointment. Especially this one. It's marked urgent."

Maybe you have to deal with those little pink or white slips of paper. Maybe by the thousands. I stuff 'em in my shirt pockets and notebook, and sometimes they stack up on my dashboard. I get back to all of them...eventually.

But this one said "Urgent." I don't get many of those.

I couldn't have known at the time that this particular return call would open up a baffling mystery that still preys on my mind in certain quiet moments. The message read: *Call Des Moines General Hospital. You have a patient in Intensive Care. Barney O'Malley wants to see you immediately.*

I held off my next client and called the IC Unit of Des Moines General, a hospital I'd been in only a couple of times. As the call was ringing in, a question worked its way to the main screen of my mind.

Who was Barney O'Malley?

I couldn't recall the name. I'd done almost twenty thousand hours of counseling over the years, and before that had worked with thousands of offenders as
a director of a correctional facility. Must be one of the guys. (But—it seems
you'd remember a name like Barney.)

The ICU nurse took my call and wanted me to come right down to the
hospital. I told her I was on my way. But first I stopped at home to see if
Barbara could help rekindle my memory.

"Barney who? O'Malley? I've no idea, Gary. You'll probably recognize him
when you see him. Would you mind picking up some rice and green onions at
the grocery store on your way home from the hospital?"

Great help.

All the way down to Des Moines General I kept bouncing the name
around in my head. I'd met a lot of interesting people in twenty years of dealing
with broken lives and shattered relationships. But Barney O'Malley? I still
couldn't place him.

A Little Strange

The ICU nurse looked up at me from her clipboard. "Dr. Rosberg? Boy, are we
glad to see you." There was genuine relief in her voice. "Barney's had a heart
attack and a stroke," she explained, "and he's been asking for you for hours.
Room Three." She motioned down the hall with a nod of her head.

I paused a moment. "Umm, ma'am, I'm a little embarrassed here. Would
you mind if I reviewed the chart before I go in? It's crazy, but—I can't quite
place the name."

She looked a little puzzled at my response, but opened the chart to reveal
the general intake information. Under the heading WHO TO CALL IN CASE
OF EMERGENCY was typed "Dr. Gary Rosberg," followed by my address and
home phone number—something I don't give out indiscriminately.

There it was, in black and white, with all the shock value of one of my old
high school report cards.

"Okay nurse," I sighed. "Point me in the right direction."

I came to Room Three and paused in the doorway. In the bed, surrounded by tubes, wires, and equipment, I saw a short, elderly man who had clearly lived a lot of life. His skin was ruddy, his teeth were worn down, and at that moment his body looked all but lifeless. The lines in his face suggested a past that hadn't been comfortable or easy.

Trouble was, I'd never seen him before in my life.

As I stepped into the room, his eyes opened with apparent recognition and his face became animated. He knew me!

"Come on in, m' boy," he rasped, and waved me closer. "Sit right down here at my bedside. Ahh, I'm so glad you came."

I sat down by the bed and looked into the old man's expectant face, feeling chills play up and down my spine. This was like one of those old episodes of "The Twilight Zone," where some guy slips into a parallel universe—everything looks the same, but then he discovers one or two details that are wildly out of place.

Who in the world was this man? And how did he know me?

Somehow I sensed he had a story to tell. If he lived to tell it.

After several minutes of small talk and showing genuine care for an apparently dying man, I worked up the nerve to expose a little of my ignorance.

"Barney, I feel a little awkward, but—I can't quite figure out how we met. Help me with that, friend."

"Well, Jerry, everyone knows you. You're *famous.*"

There were a couple of problems with his answer. First off, my name is Gary, not Jerry. But hey, give the guy a break; he was in Intensive Care with a stroke. You'd expect him to slur his words a little. But "famous"? That definitely wasn't me.

"Barney," I said, "how am I famous?"

He looked at me like I was trying to pull his leg.

"Why, *you* know, son. From politics."

Then he drawled on about meeting me at a political dinner. Since I don't go to political dinners, I was even more confused. I graciously asked which political party, and he indicated "the other one." Now I was really perplexed.

The better part of an hour passed as Barney and I talked. Actually, Barney did most of the talking as he slipped in and out of awareness.

Finally, I reached over, squeezed his hand, and stood up to leave.

"You'd better get some rest, Barney. It's been great visiting with you."

I was halfway out of the room when he called out to me.

"Young man?"

"Yes, Barney?"

"Young man, if you ever need anything—anything at all, understand?— you just call me, okay? You call old Barney."

Right through the glaze of pain and medication, I distinctly caught a twinkle in the little man's eyes.

"I'll do that, Barney," I smiled. "If I need something, I'll sure call you, my friend."

As I walked out, the nurse approached. "Dr. Rosberg, thanks for coming down. I know it meant a lot to Barney."

I could only shake my head as I walked through the hospital doors into the chill darkness of a January evening. I had just visited with a total stranger who listed my name as the person to notify in case of emergency. I was the "go-to" guy for a mystery man in his eighties who was walking on the knife-edge of eternity.

The plot thickened the next day when I called the hospital social worker.

She explained that they'd found my name on a folded up piece of paper in Barney's wallet. The paper said to call me if something happened.

"And you don't know who Barney is?" the social worker asked incredulously. "That's a little strange, isn't it?"

"Yes, ma'am," I said, "it is."

Barney had no family she knew of. He'd been taken by ambulance from a group meal site in a destitute part of town. I put a call in to the coordinator of the meal site after I hung up with a now puzzled social worker. This "information gap virus" was beginning to spread as I left confused doctors, nurses, and social workers in my wake. I really didn't have time to keep pursuing this thing, but somehow I couldn't let it go. I had to find out the link.

"You don't know Barney?" asked the meal site director with surprise in her voice. "Why, Dr. Rosberg, *everyone* knows Barney."

All right, I told myself. *Now I'm on to something!* To the woman on the phone I said, "Ma'am, tell me about him."

She gave this portrait of Barney O'Malley: A man born in Dublin, Ireland, an emigrant to America, a successful businessman and international consultant, and someone who loved to talk about his worldwide adventures. "Barney's a very important man," she told me. "He's had a run of bad luck over the last couple of years, though."

A few days ago, she added, Barney hadn't shown up for dinner at the usual time. "We went out to look for him. We were all worried. Everyone knows Barney. We saw his car in the corner of the lot, and there he was, lying in the front seat. Unconscious. Wrapped in several layers of clothes. We called an ambulance and they took him away. We all miss him, Dr. Rosberg. How's he doing?"

"I saw him last night," I told her. "I think he's in pretty tough shape, ma'am."

I hung up after a few more minutes of talking and listening to this dear woman who obviously cared deeply for a little old man named Barney O'Malley. Here was a guy who obviously had an adoring fan club of elderly folks and down-and-outers. And he thought *I* was famous.

The next day I started calling missions and homeless shelters, probing some of my old contacts from my years of working with offenders. I had several well-placed friends put the word out about Barney, but nobody seemed to know him. After several more dead ends, I still couldn't put it together. I began to wonder if I ever would.

Days turned to weeks and months, and my encounter with Barney drifted into the background. But I never forgot that twinkle in his eye and those parting words: *"Just call me if you ever need anything."* I wondered how many times he'd said those words over the years to people in his life.

The Rest of the Story

"Gary?"

Barbara spoke from across the kitchen one evening, and I looked up from my mail.

"I saw Barney O'Malley's name in the obituaries this morning," she said quietly. "He died a few days ago. Even though you never figured out who he was, I knew you'd want to know."

I didn't say anything, but I couldn't help thinking, *Now I'll never find out who he was.*

My curiosity soon got the better of me again. I still wanted to follow up on my encounter with the old man, but where would I start? Finally, I tracked down where he was living when he died, briefly shared my story, and got the name of the executor of his will. A few weeks later I put in a call to the executor.

"Barney died from a heart attack," the man told me, "but I haven't the foggiest idea how he knew you or got your phone number. How did he happen to contact you?"

For the next several minutes I shared my story with this kind, caring man who seemed as baffled as I was about Barney's connection with me.

Baffled, but not surprised.

"Barney was quite a guy, Gary. At the latter stages of his life a lot of names came out that we never knew anything about. I knew him for about ten years. At first he worked for me, and then I just kind of took care of him. That story about being from Ireland—that wasn't true at all. He was from some small town here in the Midwest. He was actually Jewish. Why he told people he was an O'Malley from Ireland we could never figure out. He was always trying to camouflage things about himself. He was quite a man though. Wouldn't hurt a flea."

He said Barney had once fathered a child—a boy—but never married. "He never saw the woman or the boy again. He lived completely alone, going from job to job, trying to make ends meet. He was quite a gentleman. His only weakness was his soft heart."

"What do you mean?" I asked him.

"People took advantage of Barney. He always denied having any living relatives, but after his death I learned he did try in his later years to contact his son. It didn't go too well, though. In fact, his son seemed interested only in getting some money or inheritance out of the deal. He showed no real interest in his dad's welfare.

"After Barney died, I went into his little apartment—out in a poor section of town. I wasn't prepared for what I saw. What a pack rat! He had seventy-five waffle irons stashed throughout the apartment, dozens of toasters, and scores of radios. You had to turn sideways to even walk through the rooms. It took me and eight men from my business a full week to empty out the place. We filled seven dumpsters full of used stuff and put a sign on it all that said, 'Take what you want.' People rummaged through and took some of it, but to be honest with you, it was pretty valueless stuff. Still, it must have meant something to Barney. I don't know—you're the counselor, not me. Can you figure it out?"

"No sir, I sure can't. Barney represents one giant puzzle to me."

A life story. A puzzling life story. And somehow, some way, it was a life story that had brushed against mine as it reached its frayed and frazzled end.

How Will Your Life Story Read?

Barney O'Malley. Who was he? How did my name come to be in his pocket, making me "next of kin" to a total stranger? God knows. Barney's life had been full of mysteries and contradictions.

But it was still a life. A life with a beginning and an end. Just like you and me, Barney was somebody. He drew breath on Planet Earth. He walked the sidewalks and streets and pathways. He smelled the flowers and felt the rain on his face. He had a past that—jumbled as it may have been—was a history, and one unique to a man named Barney O'Malley.

Just as your life story will be unique to you.

Here was a man who got up each day, earned a living, touched the lives of others, and made choices. He had feelings, dealt with stress and disappointment, and navigated a river full of changes in his lifetime. He had dreams, desires, and a destiny.

I'll probably never stop wishing I knew more about the little man who called me to his bedside on a dark January afternoon. As curious and intrigued as I may be about the life story of an indigent in Des Moines, however, there is a question that's infinitely more important to me and the people under my roof who share my name.

It's the question of *my* life story. What will it be? How will it read? How will I be remembered when I've stepped out of this life into eternity?

And yes, I have the same question for you. What will be *your* life story? In the end, what will be the legacy you leave behind? Will you leave people trying to unravel your life to determine who you really were, and what you were really all about? Will your story be as confusing as a man with a phony Irish heritage and seventy-five waffle irons in a tiny apartment?

Perhaps you live a sincere and open life. Nothing strange or hidden will be uncovered at your death. Or perhaps you live a life below the surface that's different from who you purport to be. Maybe the way Jesus described the Pharisees would even fit you, in some small way: "You are like whitewashed tombs, which look beautiful on the outside but on the inside are full of dead men's bones and everything unclean" (Matthew 23:27).

But make no mistake about it. You have a life story. Just as your father and grandfather before you and your children after you, you will leave behind a story.

As Paul wrote to his friends in Corinth, our lives are like letters that people can read. But in your heart of hearts, you may know that if you died today, your life story would be difficult to piece together. The puzzle would be missing some essential pieces. Some things just wouldn't fit. Your wife and kids and friends would try to sort through what you've left behind and be left with hurt and pain and perplexity.

Or perhaps you would leave behind a life where the pieces fit together very well. Your life would make sense to anyone looking it, and though your family would never be quite the same without you, they would go on knowing that you have preceded them to a better place with our Lord for eternity. You would show the truth of Solomon's words in Proverbs 10:7 — "The memory of the righteous will be a blessing."

Where are you? And where do you want to be?

Five Dots and a Line

During a recent dinner together, a dear friend of mine named Henry Oursler drew a simple diagram for me on the back of a napkin — an illustration with implications so vast I've only begun to deal with them. To really grasp it is to never think of your life in the same way again. David once prayed, "Show me, O Lord, my life's end and the number of my days; let me know how fleeting is my life" (Psalm 39:4). To answer that prayer, perhaps God sent a good friend to show David the same diagram Henry showed me.

What Henry drew was a line just like the one that follows this paragraph. Do you see it? Look carefully, friend, because it's a line that represents *your life*. There's an arrow at the end of it because your life actually goes on for eternity. And at the beginning of the line you'll notice five dots. The first dot represents your birth. The second dot is when you met your wife. The third is when you married, and the fourth is when you had kids. The fifth dot represents the day you will die.

····· ——————————————————————————————>

I know this sounds simplistic. You may be sitting back saying, *Well I married twice,* or *I have lots of kids,* or *I don't have any. How does this fit?* It fits. Stick with me.

You can see how close the dots are at the beginning of the line. There isn't much space between them, is there? And yet if this illustration were any more "accurate," I couldn't even portray it on a piece of paper. The dots would actually be so microscopic and close together that you couldn't even see them with the human eye. And the line on the right would stretch out beyond your imagination and comprehension.

This is a little picture of how God sees our life from an eternal perspective. He is the One who gives us the line, the line to live for eternity. So in His view, the line —not the dots—is the significant part of who we are. You and I tend to make the dots bigger than life. In actuality, many of us *live* for the dots, for our temporal life. How about you? Do you want to live for the dots, or for the line?

Here's another set of lines:

They represent my wife and my two children. The way I see it, I have a *very short* amount of time on this earth—hardly more than a heartbeat—to impact the lines of Barbara and my kids.

But that really is my job, isn't it?

It's my job to lead my family spiritually. It's my job as dad to prepare my children for living for the line. To prepare them for eternal life with God. To equip them, teach them, edify them, and—when necessary—to admonish them with deep respect and honor. As the leader of my home, my job description is clear: live for the line of eternity and lead my family the same way. It puts a different slant on this thing called "leading a family" doesn't it?

The Source of Your Story

If you're like me, you really want to have a greater impact than you've had to this point. You want to be remembered by your children as being more active in their lives than you've been to this point. You want your wife to remember you as a man who was sold out to her and only to her. You want your friends to recall you in their memories as a man who led his family well. You don't want your life story to be contradictory and puzzling at all, but very clear:

A clear commitment to your faith in Christ.

A clear commitment to your family.

A clear commitment to your friends.

If that's so, then like me, you need to follow the instruction that a father of long ago gave to his son. In one of those rare moments when two souls lock and all else fades from awareness, this concerned dad looked in his boy's eyes and said words like these:

"Son, these are the most important words I'll ever tell you: *Guard your heart,* for out of your heart will flow your life story."

That's true for me, too. Out of my heart will flow my life story. What's in my heart today and tomorrow will someday tell the story of who I really am.

It boils down to this. I need to have a plan for putting strong boundaries around my heart, if I'm going to protect it from invasion and contamination and destruction. I need to be on the alert, ready to live a life without regrets.

And—God help me—I can't do it alone.

Frankly, neither can you. Alone doesn't cut it. You and I weren't wired to keep this thing called Christian manhood in one piece by brute strength and solo effort. You want to be connected not only to your wife and kids, but also in friendship with other clear-eyed, vigilant men who are committed to finishing the race well.

I don't want to waste my short time on earth with a bunch of dead ends and wrong turns and aimless detours. I don't want my life to end up like some painful puzzle full of empty promises and faded dreams. I want a life that makes sense, a life that points toward a destiny beyond time. A life that will allow a close inspection; full of mistakes, yes, but also full of repentance and obedience. A heart that has lived life and given it all it has before it goes into an eternal relationship with our heavenly Father.

I'll bet that's what you want, too. Let's stick together then, and find out how to get it done.

Maybe, in God's providence, that's the reason I got that crazy call from Des Moines General that January afternoon. After months of pondering the strange, twisting path of a man whose life was a mystery, I find myself wanting more than ever a life so clear and straight and plain that even a child can see which way I'm pointing. "Teach me your way, O Lord; *lead me in a straight path...*" (Psalm 27:11).

Thanks, Barney, for the reminder.

If I meet you in heaven, let's have waffles together and talk.

Application Suggestions:

1. Take a few moments to write down the most important elements in your unique "life story" which you want people to remember after your death.

2. Identify any current aspect of your life which is "hidden" or "secret," and which you would regret others finding out about after your death. What must you do about it immediately in order to be living honorably, openly, and sincerely? Commit now to doing what you know you must do.

3. Use the following exercise to help you pray meaningfully about your personal and family responsibilities at this time: On a sheet of paper, draw the "five dots and a line" illustration. Write your name next to the line, and add nearby the words of Psalm 39:4. Then draw the illustration also for your family—one line each for your wife and for each of your children. Write their names by their lines, and add nearby the words of Psalm 85:7, and Psalm 90:12. Pray these verses for yourself and for your family.

4. Identify the two or three people who you think can give you the best help and encouragement at this time in guarding your heart. Write down their names and phone numbers, and make a commitment to contact at least one of them within the next three days. Tell this person your thoughts which have been prompted by reading this book, and talk about what you want to do differently in your life. Mention also why you believe you need help in doing it, and discuss how this person can help you.

To Think About & Discuss:

1. Read David's prayer in Psalm 39:4 and compare it to the prayer of Moses in Psalm 90:12. If God answered these prayers in your life, how do you think it would help you to live with a clear purpose and to avoid costly side roads and dead ends?

2. In Psalms 5:8 and 27:11, notice David's heart-cry for the Lord to show him a path in life that is "straight" or "level" or "smooth." Take a few

moments to describe what a "straight path" looks like in today's culture? What causes a straight path to go crooked?

3. How could clinging tightly to the truth of Philippians 3:12-14 keep us from becoming a "Barney O'Malley"?

4. Read Solomon's strong counsel in Proverbs 4:25-27. In what practical ways do you think God wants you to apply this counsel to your daily journey?

....

CHAPTER THREE

WHAT IT MEANS TO GUARD YOUR HEART

■

It shouldn't have happened. It *couldn't* have happened.

Yet it did.

It was outrageous, implausible, unthinkable. If anyone had dared write it into a Hollywood movie script, they'd have been laughed right out of the studio. But there it was, on page one of the morning papers.

On May 29, 1987, a nineteen-year-old West German computer analyst landed his single engine Cessna in Moscow's Red Square. He stepped out of the plane, smiled at the stunned crowds, and coolly began signing autographs.

The pilot was Mathias Rust, from Hamburg. He had navigated the Cessna 172 to Moscow from Helsinki in an unauthorized flight through over four hundred miles of the most heavily guarded airspace in the world. Shadowed at intervals by Soviet fighter planes, Rust flew on and on, unchallenged and unscathed. He penetrated the impenetrable. The protection of the former "evil empire's" sprawling frontiers had broken down in a shocking way.

The irony was rich. On the very day the Soviets were celebrating "Border

Guards Day," they failed to guard their borders. If Rust had been a cruise missile instead of a kid on a joy ride, Moscow might have been toast.

At about 7:30 in the evening, after a sixteen-hour flight, Rust approached Red Square from the south. Muscovites and tourists strolling through the great cobbled plaza looked up to see the little Cessna buzzing Lenin's tomb, then barely clearing the red brick walls of the Kremlin before finally touching down. Rust taxied to within a few feet of the Kremlin wall, just behind onion-domed St. Basil's Cathedral. The iron heart of world communism had become a landing strip for an amateur pilot with peach fuzz on his chin.

After coming to a stop, he jumped out of the plane in a jaunty red flight suit and cheerfully began greeting bystanders while authorities tried to figure out what to do. It seems there was no precedent in Soviet law for dealing with a foreign teenager who lands an airplane in Red Square.

"Something this unusual does not happen every day," said one Muscovite who saw the pilot step from his craft.

A Western diplomat in Moscow had a different slant on Rust's flight: "This puts a hole right through one of the great myths of this place, the myth of invincibility and impenetrability."

A Soviet official put it more bluntly: "There are going to be more than red faces among the military over this."

The official was right. Before the next day dawned, Party Leader Mikhail Gorbachev sacked seventy-five-year-old Defense Minister Sergei Sokolov. Several weeks later, the novice pilot on his first cross country solo flight was sentenced to four years in a Soviet labor camp.

Why did he do it?

Rust insisted he was "trying to deliver a message of peace." Whatever his reason, he became an immediate celebrity and a new German folk hero. What was next? If a single West German citizen could defy the Kremlin's vaunted defense network, how long could the Berlin Wall stand?

Broken Defenses

I can't help thinking about Mr. Rust's incredible feat when I consider Solomon's sober words in Proverbs 4:23—

> Above all else, guard your heart,
> for it is the wellspring of life.

I may think my heart is well-guarded. I may think my defenses are all in place. I may confidently assume I could *never* fall to adultery or pornography or alcoholism or any number of crippling sins or preoccupations. But on the very day I uncork the sparkling cider and celebrate "Border Guards Day" in my heart, that's the day I may be in most danger of penetration. That's the day my heart could become Satan's landing strip.

My buddy Steve Farrar tells the story about a drowning at a swimming pool in New Orleans. They found the body at the bottom of the pool. A tragedy, yes. But what made it worse was that the man drowned in the middle of a *life-guard's convention.* In the presence of hundreds of trained, tanned, athletic lifeguards eating funny little hors d'oeuvres and toasting each other for a spotless safety record, someone choked, floundered, and drowned.

It's dangerous to celebrate too early, isn't it? And it will always be too early to let down our guard until we finally step through the gates of heaven.

Let's take a closer look together at this all-important verse of Scripture. I won't pretend to be a Hebrew scholar, but I think we can zoom in on a few key elements of the verse that will help cement its truths to our lives. Are you game? Let's dive in for a few pages and go phrase by phrase.

"ABOVE ALL ELSE..."

Okay, Solomon, you've got my attention. And he *wants* my attention. "Above all else" sounds like we're getting to the punchline, doesn't it? Think of the people in your life who might say "above all else..."

- Your dad stands next to you by the station wagon as he drops you off for your first day of college. Mom has already hugged you and now sits in the car, dabbing her eyes with a kleenex. Dad grips your hand, then takes you by surprise with a rare, manly hug. He's about to cut some parental strings that have never been cut. But before he does, he looks you straight in the eyes, and says, "Son, above all else…"

- Your grandma is lying on her deathbed, and you go in to say goodbye. A familiar little smile crosses her face when she sees you. It's hard for her to speak, but you can tell she has something to say to you. These will be her last words to you in this life. The whisper is faint, but you don't want to miss a syllable. You lean close to her face and she whispers in your ear, "My dear, above all else…"

- Your coach stops you with an uplifted hand just as you and your teammates are about to charge out of the locker room for the game of your life. You've never seen the kind of intensity that burns now in his eyes. He pauses for a moment to form his words, and you sense he's trying to cram an ocean of emotion into one final sentence. "Boys, above all else…"

These three words have thrust. When we hear them, we know we're getting to the core of the message. It's truth time.

"Above all else" says that with everything in our sights, this is the thing to focus on. Let's try those instructions out on a couple of familiar situations:

You're driving your car down a residential street when you notice up ahead on your right a very little girl in pigtails wobbling alongside the road on a tiny pink bike with training wheels. It's obvious she's just learning and you wonder what in the world she's doing on the shoulder of a busy thoroughfare. You slow way down and keep your eyes on that little one as you drive by. You might be late for your appointment and you might anger the impatient driver behind you, but it doesn't matter. You're going to respect that little life…*above all else.*

Here's another one:

You're watching a game on the tube and the quarterback jams the ball into the gut of his favorite running back. It's third down, with the game on the line. The clock has ticked down to thirty seconds, and the home team is ahead by a single point deep in its own territory—where a fumble would be fatal. What's that ball carrier thinking about? Yeah, he'd like to make a first down and ice the game, but more important than that, he knows he has to protect the ball. He tucks it in and wraps both arms around it as he lowers his head and plows down field. Even when he gets hammered by a 260-pound defensive lineman he guards the ball. Why? Because guarding the ball at this point is the whole ballgame. He protects it and takes care of it…*above all else.*

Can you imagine sitting by the death bed of Solomon, the wisest man in the world, and having him say to you, "I've told you many things in our life together. I've seen it all, had it all, and experienced it all. So come close, son, and let me give you the essence of everything. Here's all you need to know boiled down to a single phrase. Above all else…

"GUARD…"

In the original language, the underlying meaning for the word "guard" suggests "exercising great care over" something.

Do you remember exercising great care over something? Maybe it was your first new car. You were so proud of it: no scratches, lots of zeros on the odometer, a heady new-car smell, and no McDonald's wrappers or old french fries under the back seat. You'd go out to the garage at night and walk slowly around it, maybe giving it a gentle little pat on the tail light.

Or maybe it's the tender observation of your infant child, asleep in the crib. Can you remember? Perhaps it wasn't so long ago. You'd find yourself going in to check on that little bundle, and then standing there a moment, looking down at that sleeping face in the glow of a Mickey Mouse nightlight. The realization steals over you that God has allowed you to be part of a miracle.

When you care deeply about something, you exercise *great care* over it.

When you care deeply about someone, you exercise *great care* over that person.

Solomon says, "Listen up: You need to exercise that kind of care over your *heart.*"

The specific term for *guard* used in this verse also has the meaning of "to guard post." Have you ever stood post? Perhaps you have, as you defended our great country in the military. Sometimes we've "stood guard" with special vigilance over our home or over our family. And it's well that we should, because that's our role as men.

When Solomon tells us to *guard*, he's talking about being alert and mindful, ready to protect and defend.

We have to both "exercise great care" and "guard post." We're the protectors of our families as well as the providers. God gave us that job. We didn't test into it, but we have it.

If you neglect to exercise great care *over your heart* or to stand post *over your heart*—if your heart is not sufficiently guarded—it will be deceived, captured, and plundered.

"YOUR HEART…"

Our heart is the very core of who we are. It's what speaks to us when we turn off the lights, lay our head on the pillow at night and try to block out the busyness of our lives. Sometimes it's the little voice of doubt that keeps us from sleeping.

Is that decision really the way to go?

Should I have walked away from that friend today? He really wanted to talk, but…I had so much to do!

I know I missed my son's game, but there will be others. My meeting was important. Those accounts don't come everyday.

The heart is everything. It's the source of all life. In our culture, we've neglected this and seen the mind as the center of everything. An ancient Hebrew might have countered, "No way. Life flows from the heart. Everything we do and everything we are—our very destiny as men—bubbles up from that deep inner spring." Used in a literal, concrete sense, the Hebrew word for "heart" meant the internal organ in the center of the chest. In its metaphorical usages, however, "heart" became the richest biblical term for the totality of man's inner or immaterial nature. This could include such forces as emotion, conscience, thought, and will.

The heart is where our life meets our environment. It's the gateway to our emotions and our relationships. It's where we feel deep joy. It's where we experience deep pain.

The Hebrews understood that a clear heart would lead to a clear head. An uncluttered heart would lead to freedom in decision-making.

And where the heart leads, the eyes, mouth, and feet will follow. "Guard your heart," Solomon says, then he continues—

> Put away perversity from your *mouth;*
>   keep corrupt talk far from your *lips.*
> Let your *eyes* look straight ahead,
>   fix your gaze directly before you.
> Make level paths for your *feet*
>   and take only ways that are firm.
> Do not swerve to the right or the left;
>   keep your *foot* from evil.

"FOR IT IS THE WELLSPRING OF LIFE"

Still with me? Let's nail one more word.

Wellspring.

What's a wellspring? I have to admit, when I began writing this book, I didn't have a good handle on that word. My dictionary defines it as "a fountainhead: the head or source of a spring, stream, or river." A second definition speaks of "a continuous, seemingly inexhaustible source or supply of something."

It's the source.

When the well dries up, you have no water.

When your heart stops pumping blood, you've lost your source of life.

When Solomon spoke of the "wellspring of life," he was talking about the core of who we are. It's the artesian source of *our very selves*. And—above all else —we've got to guard that source and keep it from deadly contamination.

Let me take you back to another day in recent history. It's not as dramatic, perhaps, as a Cessna touching down in Red Square, but for a few well-placed French executives, it couldn't have been worse if someone had hijacked the Eiffel Tower.

Contaminated at the Source

It was early 1990 when this panic occurred. It was a scare with international implications, but it wasn't war, famine, or earthquake.

On February 9, Ron V. Davis, president of Perrier Group of America Inc. in Greenwich, Connecticut, ordered Perrier, that chic fizzy water, removed from distribution in North America. It seems that a lab in North Carolina had picked something up in one of those trademark green bottles: traces of benzene, a toxic chemical known as a carcinogen. The product that flowed from the purest, most perfect wellspring of all, the artesian wells, had been tainted.

A few days later, on February 14, most romanticists turned their hearts toward their Valentines. But in Paris, the city of love, many hearts were beating at record rates for a different reason. At a press conference the folks at Source Perrier announced a worldwide recall of *160 million bottles* of their famous product.

The unprecedented global recall cost the French company about $30 million up front. This didn't include the fear that if they couldn't bounce back after the scare, it would threaten the industry of "bottled pure water." You have to admit, when you pay a couple bucks for a bottle of water, your expectations are a little high. I mean—excuse the suggestion—you *could* get it out of the tap. Then to learn that it not only isn't pure, but it's also potentially contaminated and cancer causing. That's a tad unsettling.

The North Carolina lab identified benzene in the Perrier at 15 parts per billion—way beyond the USFDA limit of 5 parts per billion. How could it happen? Eventually, company officials explained that workers had failed to change filters that usually took out the benzene that is naturally present in carbon dioxide, the gas used to make Perrier bubbly.

The product of the wellsprings, the heart of the purest water in the world, had been contaminated during the bottling process—and now, what would be the ripple effect? No Perrier, no parties? What would people drink with their oysters?

I have to admit I didn't lose much sleep over this crisis. I never liked the stuff. But I guess the big news here is that careless workers in an unguarded moment allowed this impeccable beverage to become tainted. And that careless-ness touched lives all over the world.

In Proverbs 4:23, Solomon is telling us that (above all else!) we must guard that deep inner source of life from contamination. If we do not, everything that flows out of our lives from now on will be colored and tainted by the toxins we've allowed to seep into the very source of who we are. It will effect everything we touch: our marriage, our kids, our job, our friends, and our potential ministry for the Lord.

Tragically, some of those deadly toxins can go on poisoning lives and families even after we've departed from earth. I'm thinking about a lady named Brenda, and her late husband, Jim. On a warm summer evening six weeks after her husband's death, Brenda ventured out to Jim's tool shed to gather some of his things for a yard sale. That's when she encountered some boxes of his stuff tucked away amongst the oil cans, hedge clippers, and work gloves. What she found were pictures of her husband. Scores of them. Yet he wasn't alone. There were women in the pictures, too—too many to count. The scenes and acts and poses those pictures portrayed seared into Brenda's stunned, unbelieving mind. Try as she might in later years, she could not wash them from her memory.

What may have started out for Jim as an adolescent dabbling with pornog-raphy had become a hideous adult obsession. Here were pictures—horrible, degrading pictures—of the man she'd trusted and loved. She had borne his children, cooked his meals, slept in his bed. She had clung to him during the hard times, walked the beach with him in romantic moments, stood at his side at Little League games and their kids' birthday parties. Her goal in life had simply been to grow old with her husband.

But it wasn't to be. When the pain of Jim's secret became more than he could bear, he "missed a turn" while speeding on a crooked highway. No one could say for sure, but the circumstances looked a lot like suicide.

In a heartbeat, he was gone.

But the well had been poisoned long ago.

Even after Brenda remarried, the bitter toxins tainted her memories, clouded her moods, and cast long shadows over a new relationship. Brenda still experienced the pain of her first husband's betrayal, and her second husband felt the impact of another man's actions from years before.

Sin isn't an easy thing to lock in a back closet, is it? Sooner or later, it has a way of getting out. Its poison seeps through doors and walls like nuclear waste in a landfill. Sin birthed in our hearts can spread not only across our own personal landscape, but into the souls and minds of those around us.

Worth Protecting

That's the reason for Solomon's warning, and that's the reason for this book. Above all else, we need to protect the deep well of our hearts. Because what flows out of that well will determine the very story of our lives.

Like me, I'm betting you want to finish the race well. As you look around at the wreckage and unbelievable pain of men who fell asleep on sentry duty, you want to make sure your name doesn't show up on the casualty list. You want the kind of defenses that will protect some things in your life that are worth protecting. Like me, you may be a little frightened at the thought of an enemy landing in your heart.

We don't want Satan riding a cruise missile over our walls.

Or even a Cessna.

Let's help each other guard our hearts.

Application Suggestions:

1. Select one area of life in which you may be most susceptible to "letting down your guard"—an area where you might tend to feel over-confident. On paper, list the *reasons* you feel strong in this area. Then analyze each reason you listed. Are these reasons really as good as you thought?

2. *Why* is it important to guard your heart? Make a list (and number each item in priority order) of *your own* personal reasons in answer to this question.

3. Identify a person you regard as setting a good example in guarding his or her heart. What evidence leads you to this impression about this person? Determine now to more closely watch and learn from this person's example.

4. Make a list of the most dangerous "contaminants" which you must guard your own heart against. Then take the list to God in prayer, and ask Him to show you in the days and weeks ahead how you can guard against these dangers.

To Think About & Discuss:

1. Read Proverbs 4:23, then restate the verse in your own words. What phrase grips you the most, and why?

2. Look at the "contaminants" you listed in Application Suggestion 4 above. Prioritize these in order according to their degree of "potency" in our lives today.

3. Compare Proverbs 4:23 with Proverbs 4;13 and 7:2. Besides our heart, what else does Solomon say we should "guard"?

4. What does Jesus tell us to guard against? Look at Matthew 16:6 and 16:11-12, Mark 13:32-37, and Luke 12:15.

···

CHAPTER FOUR

Castles Under Fire

■

Ever built a sand castle?

It's something like this...

You're just a little guy. You've begged for weeks, and your parents finally relent and take you to the beach. Dad's preoccupied with making sure everything gets packed and with getting there in time to nab the perfect parking place. You jump out of the car before it quite stops moving, sand bucket and shovels in hand, striped towel flowing in the wind. Just as you head for the water you hear your mom yelling, "Put on some lotion or the sun'll kill you." Your dad's still grousing about getting there "too late" and having to park in the auxiliary lot. Getting out of the car, he looks a little like Fred McMurray playing "Mr. Hobbes Takes a Vacation." His legs look like they haven't seen the sun since the Civil War. Let's face it, this beach thing just isn't his strong suit.

Facing the sun, Mom smears on coconut oil and settles in to acquire the sort of deep, rich tan displayed by the ladies in her magazines. Your adolescent sister, decked out in the latest swimsuit, pretends she's never seen you in her life, and parks with her transistor radio a hundred yards down the beach. True to form, your little brother is ready to be a pest and bug you, just like you always did with your sister.

Fine.

None of this matters. You've waited for this moment and now, *you're ready.*

You've finally made it to the beach. And nothing is going to get in the way of building…YOUR CASTLE.

With pinpoint accuracy you identify the reach of the tide. You plop into the warm sand at precisely the right place to allow enough space and time to construct your castle before the ocean sweeps in. (How do little boys know this stuff? I don't know. It's a male thing, I think.) As you position yourself in the sand, a vision swims grandly into your mind's eye…

The coolest castle ever built by man or boy.

First the main building, then the protective walls, and finally the moat. Soldiers and horsemen abound, the sentries are in place to kill the bad guys, and maybe—just maybe—there will be a damsel in distress in the tower next to the hunchbacked bellringer.

Castles.

You build 'em and they entertain you for hours. All right, so you get a little sunburn on your back, some sand in your bologna sandwich, and your baby brother sits on a few of your walls. These things can be endured. Because you know that as the day wears on, you're approaching a glorious, inevitable conclusion. The oncoming tide advances on your castle, inch by inch, threatening destruction and mayhem. The grim defenders stand their posts, faithful to the end. Finally, a finger of foam brushes against the wall, and you know it's coming —just a wave or two away. Armageddon! Then the fateful wave arrives and smashes into your fortress with the velocity of an A-bomb. *All right!* Proud towers crumble. Mighty walls melt away. Soldiers pitch headlong from their posts and the king tumbles from his high throne. As the wave retreats, all that's left is a tell-tale mound. That too, will disappear, leaving only a memory of the finest castle you've ever constructed.

But the waves can never sweep away the memory, can they? Memories are forever. Which is precisely why we should make as many good ones as we can, while we can.

But castles weren't built only by skinny little boys on beaches. Since we're doing a little looking back, let's climb into the time machine and zoom further back for a look at some real castles, castles of the Middle Ages.

Two Ways to Take a Castle

True castles—the private fortresses—first appeared in northwest Europe in the ninth century. Many of the remnants are still there. The long waves of time have not yet swept them away. One authority catalogs the remains of at least fifteen hundred castles in England alone.

Did you ever wonder who lived in those things? Besides the lord and his family, the household of a castle included knights, squires, men-at-arms, a porter who kept the outer door, and watchmen. There was also a ministerial and domestic staff, a steward who administered the estate, and any number of servants. The larger the land holdings of course, the larger the staff. But one thing was always true: The castle was built to protect.

Show me a castle, and I'll show you a history of warfare. Family strongholds were typically built on high ground, positioned to command a stretch of navigation or a mountain pass. They were placed in strategic positions in order to protect the holdings of the lord as well as the family within. Boiled down, medieval military science was basically the science of "the attack and defense of castles." As castles were constructed to defend, opponents became increasingly determined to attack. As the sophistication of the defenses grew, so did the schemes of the attackers.

There were two ways to attack a castle. The most overt was the *frontal assault*. That's where you roll right up to the walls and start hammering away with catapults, battering rams, flaming arrows, and hordes of invaders scrambling up long ladders. This head-on approach was an attempt to simply overpower the castle by main strength.

Failing that tactic, the second approach might be employed: a *sneak attack*. These sorts of tactics were only limited by the deviousness of an enemy's imagination.

So if castles were built to shield and enemies plotted to attack, how were the inhabitants within the walls protected?

With a plan.

The architects of castles had a plan to protect the families within. It started with the construction of the wall around the castle. The castle's main line of resistance was the curtain wall with its projecting towers. The ground in front of the curtain was kept free of all cover. If there was a moat, the ground was cleared well beyond it. Some castles consisted of a walled enclosure a hundred feet wide by fifty feet deep, with a powerful cylindrical tower at the corner. Some large castles kept a year's supply of food. A garrison of sixty men could hold out against an attacking force ten times its number. Feeding sixty men from a well-stocked granary supplemented by cattle, pigs, and chickens brought in at the enemy's approach might be far easier than feeding six hundred men from a war-ravaged countryside.

Let's look more closely at these two approaches to storming a castle.

Storming the Stronghold

Frontal attacks included the use of mobile assault towers, normally assembled at the battle site. The goal was to provide the storming party with both cover and height to allow them advantages in the assault. The towers would also provide cover for battering rams to be used to bash and splinter the front gate. Archers with crossbows shot fire-bearing arrows and torches. Attackers scrambling up long ladders would engage the castle's protectors in hand-to-hand combat. Catapults would fling fifty pound rocks as far as two hundred yards.

The strategic placement and soaring walls of the fortress gave it an imposing look, and the defenses were usually sufficient to turn back most head-on assaults. But if the enemy was ingenious enough to learn that the direct approach wouldn't lead to success, they would be more creative, looking for ways to conquer the castle through "a back door."

If you can't knock down the walls, what do you do? Starve 'em out! Cut off their provisions, or—worse yet—intercept their water supply. If the enemy could cut off or spoil the stronghold's "wellspring," it was only a matter of time before they could win their objective.

In the First Crusade, when the Turks besieged the Crusaders in a castle at Nicaea and cut off their water supply, the beleaguered Christians suffered terrible hardships, eventually drinking their horses' blood and each other's urine, and burying themselves in damp earth in hope of absorbing the moisture. After eight days without water, the Christians surrendered, and were killed or sold as slaves.

One of the most frequent weaknesses of a castle could be found in the very ground upon which it was built. Typically, a stronghold would be raised on solid rock, but if location was deemed more important to the lord and builder than the structural strength of the foundation below the castle walls, then the *subsoil* could be a prime enemy target. A castle built on anything less than solid rock was open to attack by digging beneath its walls. The invaders would typically tunnel beneath a wall, preferably under a corner or tower, supporting the tunnel roof with heavy timbers as the sappers advanced. When they reached a point directly under the wall, the timbering was set ablaze, collapsing earth and masonry above.

The process wasn't as easy as it sounds. In 1215, when King John laid siege to Rochester Castle, a vast square keep defended by rebel knights, he ordered nearby Canterbury to manufacture "by day and night as many picks as you are able." Six weeks later, the digging had progressed enough that John commanded the home front to "send to us with all speed by day and night the fattest pigs of the sort least good for eating, to bring fire beneath the tower." When the poor porkers were torched, the lard produced a sufficient blaze in the mine to destroy the timbering and bring down a great section of the wall of the keep. Rumor has it that the victory was followed by a barbecue.

Another way to undermine the inhabitants was to take them by surprise with a ruse. (Remember the Trojan horse?) Deceptions might include attackers dressing as peasants and surprising the castle inhabitants once inside, or faking truces to gain the gates and wreck bloody havoc. At other times, the assailants would find ways to bribe the defenders and persuade them to defect.

Sennacherib tried that ploy while he was besieging King Hezekiah and the walls of Jerusalem.

> Then the Assyrian ambassador shouted in Hebrew to the people on the wall, "Listen to the great king of Assyria! Don't let King Hezekiah fool you. He will never be able to save you from my power. Don't let him fool you into trusting the Lord to rescue you. Don't listen to King Hezekiah. Surrender! You can live in peace

here in your own land until I take you to another land just like this one—with plentiful crops, grain, wine, olive trees, and honey. All of this instead of death! (2 Kings 18:28-32, TLB)

Show me a castle worth taking, and I'll show you a history of attackers with ingenious plots.

Your Battle

Just for a moment, imagine yourself the lord in your own castle. You hired the best architect available to help you structure your fortress. Now it's complete, your family is tucked snugly within, and you're satisfied. Quite frankly, it looks pretty good. The walls are high and impressive, and your bright banners snap smartly in the wind. Your kids are playing in the courtyard, your wife is busy and fulfilled, and you are leading effectively. It's a good life.

Suddenly your peace is shattered by a hail from a sentry in one of the towers. Something strange is going on across the field, in the shadows of the forest that surrounds your fortress. A glint of sunlight on speartips. The unmistakable blowing and stamping of horses. Smoke rising from an outlying village. A prickly feeling of apprehension and danger.

It appears your little domain is about to be attacked.

Sure enough, it comes.

Sometimes the raids are at night, sometimes in high daylight. Wave after wave. Enemies rain arrows on your refuge with a keen eye and ruthless heart. Battle towers roll slowly toward your walls, and just outside arrow range, a catapult is being readied.

Quickly hustling your wife and kids to a safe place in the belly of the fortress, you mount the walls to assess your enemy's strength. Suddenly the whole castle resounds to the sickening thud of a massive battering ram, smashing into your gates. You know that your gate's huge, handpicked timbers are thick, but…how long can they endure such punishment? Several days? Several hours?

And what might that enemy of yours be up to while you're trying to deal with the frontal attack? Could he be building trenches underneath the walls?

Might he be planning a fire that could engulf the once safe environment you built for your family? And what about your servants inside the walls? Could someone have invaded the security and betrayed you from within? The questions race through your mind as your defenders scramble to their posts and look to you for direction.

It's too late to rebuild the castle, isn't it? Any construction shortcuts will soon be revealed in the heat of battle. Those areas where you tried to save a few coins and shave a couple of weeks off the construction time will become all too obvious.

Yes, it's too late to change the structure…but it's not too late to fight the battle. Fight you must, with all your heart and soul, because this is a battle for the very survival of your family.

Men on the Ramparts

This little sketch of medieval warfare isn't really all that much different than the battle you and I find ourselves in today as we seek to protect our families. Let's face it, we're at war in this country. Our culture is attacking on every front. The wise man not only has "built his house upon the rock," but is well prepared to stand against the onslaught. If we're going to fight the battle, we need to know not only our own strengths, but also the weapons of the enemy. We need to know where men are getting hammered.

Just prior to writing this book, I surveyed over a thousand "knights" throughout our land, asking them where their own hearts and family castles seemed most at risk. The results, I believe, may confirm some things you're already experiencing. And that's my point: You aren't alone. You don't have to fight this battle by yourself, but you must fight it! Your life story and the survival of your family depend on it.

I started my survey with my home state of Iowa, but I wanted to go beyond the familiar heartland. So I threw my net out wider, enlisting the help of guys from British Columbia to Texas, from South Carolina and Tennessee to California. The men in my survey ranged from single men to newly married guys to seasoned citizens. Men from their twenties to their seventies. Men without children, men with kids, and men with grandkids. Professional men, laborers, pastors, and students. Men from a wide range of ethnic backgrounds, financial means, and church affiliations.

But all these men had one thing in common: They were all "regular guys" trying to lead their homes and yearning to finish the race as a knight of one lady. I listed potential threats to their "castle" that men might experience, then asked each of the men to rate these threats, both in the area of frontal assaults (external threats) as well as sneak attacks (internal threats), which they encounter day to day in their lives as Christian men.

As you read what I learned, take a moment to rank these threats according to your own experience.

Frontal Attacks: The External Threats Facing Men

Frontal Attack #1—CAREER PRESSURES

It may come as no surprise that careers and work-related pressures rated as the number one threat to the castles of the men in my survey. Thirty percent of the respondents rated keeping a balance between career and home as the top challenge facing their lives.

Frontal Attack #2—DISTRACTIONS

The second major threat—and close on the heels of the first—was the distractions of finances, power, and accumulation of stuff. Distractions were rated 28 percent of the time by the men in my survey.

Frontal Attack #3—RELATIONSHIP PRESSURES

The pressures men feel in maintaining healthy relationships came in third, with 24 percent of the men inking that box on the survey. This would include relationships with parents, wives, kids, and coworkers.

Frontal Attack #4—SEXUAL TEMPTATION

The fourth assault on our castles, sexual temptation, was reported by 18 percent of the respondents as a significant threat to them as men.

Sneak Attacks: The Internal Threats Facing Men

Sneak Attack #1—THE SEARCH FOR SIGNIFICANCE

Thirty percent of the men rated their "search for significance" as the first and foremost threat to their castle. This represents our desire to impact our culture, to do and *be* something. When 30 percent of the men rate this as the major internal struggle they face, it only reinforces the belief that men define who they are by their impact on the world.

Sneak Attack #2—PASSIVITY

I found it intriguing that 29 percent rated the tendency to be passive as the second internal threat to their castle. When you have 30 percent of the men wanting to make an impact in life, and then combine that with 29 percent reporting their tendency to be passive, it's clear why so many men struggle! On one hand, they want desperately to make a difference; on the other, they find themselves withdrawing. It's a curious and potentially stressful combination.

Sneak Attack #3—CONTROL

Twenty-seven percent of the men in my survey rated their tendency to want to be in control as the third major internal struggle they faced. Men like to be in charge.

Sneak Attack #4—COMPETITION

Fourteen percent rated competition, the very component that so often defines us, as fourth on their list. Men compete. And the men in my survey indicated that the desire to compete can threaten their castles when it breaks out of certain boundaries.

One Man Under Siege

It's not easy dealing with multiple attacks on our castle walls! Most men like to be focused on one thing at a time. If there's a pesky battering ram trying to smash down the front gates, who's got time to deal with a bunch of guys with shovels around back trying to dig under the wall? We like to handle our pressures one by one, don't we? Unfortunately, life doesn't work that way.

If we're overly focused on work, our relationships may suffer. If we're trying to nail a budget down, we might become very controlling, or—just as bad— become passive and crawl into our escape hatches. If we get too competitive while trying to grab for significance in our lives, we may set ourselves up for sexual temptation.

The bottom line is that trying to keep all these things in balance isn't easy. And that's why we need to be on guard. That's why we need to stay alert.

I recently received a letter from a man who almost slept through the most crucial battle of his life. By the time he woke up, it was late in the day—very late. But at least he woke up!

I was flying home after speaking at a marriage conference with over a thousand people in attendance. I didn't have a moment to myself that weekend until I finally buckled into my airline seat for the long flight home. Closing in on a welcome cat-nap, I suddenly remembered the letter I'd stuffed into my coat pocket. A man had pressed it into my hand as I was trying to talk to two or three other couples. (It can be a zoo sometimes at these conferences!) Now, in the comparative peace of the Chicago-bound 737, I drew it out, and read these words:

> Hey Rosberg.
>
> Caught your conference this weekend. You had some pretty powerful stuff to lay on us. I have to admit, I walked in on Friday night pretty stinking arrogant. But that isn't how I left.
>
> I'm thirty-six. Married for twelve years. Been a Christian since high school. What big problems could I have? My wife asked me to go to this conference last year and I held her off. Too much work on my plate. This year I asked *her* to go because even I thought we needed a tune-up.
>
> She was a bit hesitant. It wasn't until Saturday night that she filled in the blanks on that one. I thought, "Hey, this will be okay. We might even learn a thing or two about communicating on a deeper level." Let me make one thing clear: I love my wife, Gary. I

just don't have the map to lead my home. I've been real busy lately but she understands. Or so I thought...

Gary, there's been a lot of what you called "erosion." She's filled her life with the kids, work, and other stuff. I thought we were rolling along pretty well. Until Saturday night. Now I'm truly scared, Rosberg. I usually go to God for the big ticket items, but try to handle the low maintenance stuff myself. Well, I blew it. What I thought was low maintenance was anything but.

This lady's hurting. In fact, she may be beyond hurting. To put it like you would, it was like sitting in the dugout half asleep the whole game. Suddenly, you're at the plate with the tying run at third, two out, you've got two strikes and the ball is halfway to the plate before you even wake up to the fact there's a game going on!

So you throw your bat at it and get a piece of it. That moment lasts forever. *Dear God, let him drop that ball and just give me one more swing. I know I can drill it to left field and at least tie this thing.* Don't worry, Rosberg, I haven't given up yet. But it may be a long time before I know whether I'll get that last swing.

Gary, I thought I was doing okay. Not a great leader of the home, but not bad. What I learned was that I'm ready to miss the bus home and get left at the ballpark. In just three days at your conference I learned what a mess I've made of my life. Now I'm facing the reality of losing my wife and kids! How is it possible that I had my values and priorities so screwed up? The $64,000 question is really this: If I get another shot at this marriage, how am I going to stay in the game and stop myself from reverting to the old habits?

What I'm trying to say, in a round about way, is thanks for the "wake up call." For whatever it's worth, you really made me stop and think about how to live my life.

Now catch the last few lines of this beleaguered knight's letter:

You know what tears me apart, Gary? My wife asked me to go to your conference *last year*. But I didn't hear her. I had to beg her to go this year, and she didn't want to listen to me. If only I'd had a guy like you last year to look me in the eye and say, "Don't be stupid. Go to the conference." This has been the longest night of my life. Whatever spare prayers you may have I would greatly appreciate.

How's Your Castle Standing Up?

After reading this letter, you may be heading downstairs to the kitchen to check on your wife. Or you may be putting this book down to give her a call from your hotel room on the road. Just to make sure she's still there. The wake-up call from my friend may have gotten your attention.

Or you may miss the signal and stay on automatic pilot. For one reason or another, you may not be ready for the message. Or perhaps you're flooded with memories from the hurt you've experienced in your past when you missed that "last pitch," and now you have to live with the painful results.

Here are three things we can count on:

One, we all have castles that need leading.

Two, we all need help and encouragement in leading them.

And three, if your heart and home haven't come under assault in the past—whether from frontal assault or sneak attack—*it's coming*.

Some men in the battle today are getting hammered, but they're ready. They've built their castle with a plan on a strong foundation, they've been keeping watch on the walls, and they've filled the cellar with adequate supplies to last through the duration of the battle. The knight and his lady are in sync as they face the attacks that shake their castle walls.

If you're one of them—then high five!

Other men haven't got the plan intact, but they're at war. If this is you, here's the word: It's too late to rebuild your castle, but much too early to surrender.

Besides, you have more resources than you know—and a few secret weapons to boot. Read on, and you'll see what I mean.

Application Suggestions:

1. As preparation for reading the rest of the book, write down the four "frontal attacks" and the four "sneak attacks" mentioned in this chapter. Then rank them in order of their personal danger to you, based on your own experience.

2. Look again at the letter quoted in this chapter from the husband who heard the author speak at a marriage conference. Count down to the seventh paragraph, (the one beginning "Gary, I thought I was doing okay"). Rewrite this paragraph to make it a true description of you and your marriage.

3. Think about a time in the past when your "castle" came under attack. In one sentence, how would you describe and summarize that attack? To protect your home and marriage, how did you respond? What lessons did you learn from this experience?

4. From what you've learned and thought about so far from reading this book, what do you most want to communicate to your wife? Decide now on a time and a way to tell her these things.

To Think About & Discuss:

1. Review the principles of spiritual warfare in 2 Corinthians 10:3-5. Would you say these are offensive tactics, defensive tactics, or both?

2. The author writes in this chapter, "Our culture is attacking on every front. The wise man not only has 'built his house upon the rock,' but is well prepared to stand against the onslaught." Take a fresh look at the word picture Jesus gave about the house built on rock in Matthew 7:24-27. (Don't allow your familiarity with these words to rob you of the impact of this crucial teaching.) In specific terms, how can a man living today build his house—and his life—on the rock of Christ's words?

3. Read again Paul's stirring battle cry in Ephesians 6:10-18. As you consider these verses, what are three practical things you can begin doing right away to put this teaching to work in your life?

4. Thinking again of what you see in Ephesians 6:10-18 (and elsewhere in Scripture), what can you reasonably expect in your life if you do *not* obey the command in verse 10?

....

CHAPTER FIVE

FRONTAL ATTACK #1:

CAREER PRESSURES

•

The men reading this book with you work in every job imaginable.

They're laborers, salesmen, teachers, and pastors. They may work the farm or the spreadsheets. They're self-employed, looking for employment, or retired from employment. They're physicians who treat us when we're sick, counselors who salve wounded hearts, mechanics who repair broken engines. Some are in their first job and others in their umpteenth.

But one thing we all have in common: We were designed by our heavenly Father *to work*. We're called to work—that's been true from the beginning of time. Remember the original setup?

> Now the Lord God had planted a garden in the east, in Eden, and there he put the man he had formed.... The Lord God took the man and put him in the Garden of Eden to work it and take care of it. (Genesis 2:8-15)

We men have been in partnership with God from the start, and He wants us to work in order to provide for our family. Work is good. Work is God's design. Psalm 104:22-23 gives the timeless picture:

> The sun rises...
> Then man goes out to his work,
> to his labor until evening.

So if work is good and right and necessary, then why is it that the men in my survey rated work as the number one force endangering their castle? When men acknowledge the need to guard their heart, why do they mention jobs and careers as the biggest threat of all? How and why do we become so overwhelmed?

Before I talk about our struggle in this area, let me tell you about a job I had recently. It was a job that came out of nowhere, a job that required every muscle group in my body and taxed my mind and emotions beyond anything I've experienced before or since.

It was the best job I've ever had.

My Best Job

Usually people in Iowa remember summers for the sticky heat. But not the summer of 1993. That summer will always be remembered for the rain that never seemed to end. The rain began falling in Iowa in late spring, and by July 1 several times the usual amount of precipitation had fallen. Farmers couldn't work their crops. Mothers couldn't scoot their kids out to the playgrounds. And each day the earth's soil was becoming more and more saturated.

In the midst of the incessant downpours, I was headed to Atlanta to attend the Christian Booksellers Convention. Publishers, songwriters, recording artists, and authors would be meeting with booksellers from around the country, and I had an idea for a book I wanted to talk about with the right people. So like thousands of other people I found myself shouldering my garment bag at Atlanta International, looking for a hotel shuttle.

Ten seconds after flopping down on my hotel bed, I did what any red-blooded American male would do—I grabbed the TV remote. As soon as CNN appeared on the screen, I was immediately home again. Just that quick. The lead news story zoomed in on terrible flooding in *my suburb* of West Des Moines. Videotapes showed workers laboring feverishly in the torrential rains, sandbagging the water treatment plant and the river banks.

I couldn't believe my eyes. There before me were the submerged landmarks of my hometown. National Guardsmen were on patrol. Meanwhile, the meteorologists were predicting more rain.

I called home to see how my girls were doing. The phone rang the customary five times before kicking into the answering machine. But the recording wasn't the chipper voices of my two girls as it usually was. It was Barbara's voice saying wearily, "We can't answer the phone right now. The girls and I are out sandbagging the river. Please call back later."

Now I found myself shifting from shock to fear. Here I was in a classy Atlanta hotel, absentmindedly chewing on one of the fancy green-foiled mints sitting on my nightstand. And my wife and two girls were sandbagging the river. There was something wrong with that picture. I needed to go home. Fast. My place was in Des Moines to encourage and lead my family through what would turn out to be one of the most incredible experiences of our lives.

I caught a quick flight home and looked out the window as we flew over downtown Des Moines. There were no cars, no people—only water. Everywhere. The city had become a bona fide disaster area. All commerce had ceased. Floodwaters surged through buildings, cars, houses, schools, parks, and streets, leaving huge populations without drinking water.

Barbara met me at the airport. I could see the strain in her eyes and face. She was ready to pass the torch of family leadership to where it belonged: to me. She'd done an admirable job leading the charge. She did what she had to do, just like every other family in the flood zones. She helped combat the river with her hands and injured her back filling sandbags. She prayed with our daughters and gave the girls the necessary emotional support to assure them all would be okay.

But it was my job to lead the family again.

After being home for less than an hour, we got a call from a friend whose shop was about to be swallowed by the river. Now it was my turn to serve. Before I got off the phone, Barb was putting on her sandbagging clothes. I just followed her example. So the Rosbergs, along with dozens of others, evacuated the shop amid tears, hugs, and incredible teamwork.

On the way home from my first flood job, I received a call from my office that the swirling waters had separated one of my clients from his home. Along with hundreds of others, he was now a resident of an elementary school gymnasium turned Red Cross Shelter just six blocks from my home.

National Guard troops, moms and dads, kids, and Red Cross volunteers were there working side by side. Nameless heroes served each other. Flood victims, dazed and disoriented, came in droves. Barb and I helped where we were needed. Our first assignment was to fill out forms registering volunteers. Twenty minutes later, I was charged with establishing a counseling program for flood victims in a second Red Cross shelter three blocks away in a local church.

In only a few hours my life had taken a 180-degree turn from an elegant hotel in Atlanta to this disaster zone in Des Moines.

During these painful days I sat with elderly men and women who had lost everything: their furniture, their clothes, their family photograph albums, their security. I listened to stories of loss, despair, and hope. I saw a community pull together.

But the strain could be overwhelming. I personally "hit the wall" when I stormed a Red Cross truck that had delivered a plate of cookies to the kids in my shelter. The problem wasn't the delivery. The problem was that they had given them out at our shelter by accident, and now they intended to take them back. A little boy tugged on my shirt. "Dr. Gary," he said, "they're taking our cookies away." I began muttering to myself, "They aren't going to take your cookies. They aren't going to take these children's cookies." Before I knew it, I was walking through the shelter with a pack of kids behind me chanting in unison, *"They aren't going to take our cookies. They aren't going to take our cookies."* Next thing I remember, I was standing in the back of a truck, nose to nose with three Red Cross volunteers, one of them a friend from college over twenty years ago.

"I'm taking back the cookies," I snarled. "These kids have lost everything— but you are *not* taking the cookies!"

I got the cookies.

Working Right

It's summer again in Iowa, one year after the Flood of '93. I live in the same house, write in the same study, drive the same streets. But something is different. We're not a community in crisis today. Just a year ago it was raining incessantly. Today it's hot and sunny, and people are going about their day, planning bike rides, picnics, and tomorrow's Father's Day celebrations. Last year at this time we were planning how to get enough water to drink, which place in the river to sandbag, and where to find a place to take a shower.

I'll never forget that summer. The experience of serving men, women, and kids during the flood will remain vivid in my memory the rest of my life. I was shoulder to shoulder with thousands of others, helping to serve meals and hand out clothes. I mediated disputes, ministered to guardsmen, and counseled elderly people fearful of leaving the wreckage of their homes. I sat in decision-making meetings with the Christian Relief Effort, a group of churches banding together to help meet the needs of flood survivors. I helped clean out debris from houses, and went back weeks later and painted those houses.

And I can truthfully say it was the best job I've ever had.

But why?

I know it sounds like a contradiction. I have to admit, even as I tap out these words on my computer, that I'm a little surprised to remember it as such a great job. It was hard, painstaking work that never seemed to end. I felt more emotionally drained than ever in my entire life. I have never been more physi-cally tired. Every muscle in my body ached from the strain and stress, the exertion and fatigue. My gifts and stamina were taxed to the max. Why was it the best job? Why was it so satisfying?

Because I was working as God said we should work—with all my heart. "Whatever you do, work at it with all your heart, as working for the Lord, not for men, since you know that you will receive an inheritance from the Lord as a reward. It is the Lord Christ you are serving" (Colossians 3:23-24).

Whatever it is you do, my friend, God wants you doing it with all your heart. That includes your work, which is one way we serve God. You may be the governor of your state or the man who cleans his office. You may work the farm, travel the road, or build houses. It doesn't matter *what* you do. What matters is *how* you do it.

It all comes down to your heart. How do you serve? Willingly? Reluctantly? Selfishly?

When we do a job, any job, we are standing for Christ—and the world is watching. We are His representatives. That's the reason we need to be whole-hearted in whatever we do. Think about the non-Christians you work with. Do you think they ever observe your work? After hearing your claim of being different, don't you think they wonder if you really *are* different?

They're watching, all right, with all sorts of motives. Some with hardened hearts may watch to see you trip up. Others hope beyond hope that the Lord you say is real can become real to them, and they look at you to learn how He can be.

Todd learned this truth up close with a coworker named Brett.

Todd's Story

Todd's a Christian man with a heart for Christ and for impacting others. He had tried to share his faith with coworkers, but Brett had put the skids on the talk, having had some "bad experiences with church" as a kid.

Todd and I had lunch one day, and he told me about a dilemma he was facing in a project he was working on with Brett. Todd had bid the job, and now realized he had significantly underestimated the cost. It was his responsibility to clean it up. The heat was on as Todd had to make a judgment call. Should he go back to the customer and face up to possibly losing the contract by informing them of the problem, or should he manipulate the numbers and squeak by?

Todd knew Brett was watching. Would Todd's faith make a difference? Was it for real, or just a convenience in good times? Who would Todd serve? His own pride by covering his misjudgment? Or his Lord by facing it honestly?

The honor of God was on the line. Todd remembered what Paul wrote about others watching your work in 1 Thessalonians 4:11—"Make it your ambition to lead a quiet life, to mind your own business and to work with your hands, just as we told you, so that your daily life may win the respect of outsiders…." Paul knew that outsiders will be watching those who claim to be Christians. Paul also knew that hard work was a witness for Christ to those searching for the Truth.

As Todd and I looked at his situation in this biblical context, the conclusion was a no-brainer. Todd made the right call. He went back to the customer and faced the music. And Brett responded by wanting to know why.

"You see, Brett," Todd told him, "this faith thing is more than heading to church on Sundays. It also impacts how I live, how I work…"

The Lord tells us to work *for Him* in everything we do. Why? So we can be a window for others to see Him through us. We serve Him. Not always perfectly. But willingly.

Work can become satisfying because we know that in serving others we are really *serving Jesus Christ!* And life doesn't get any better than that.

How Do We Learn This Stuff Anyway?

I don't know where you learned to work. I learned from my dad, and he learned from his dad. My parents had a family business, an industrial laundry. All four of their kids worked summers, weekends, and even holidays. When others took vacations, our family worked. Why? Because the elderly in the nursing homes and the sick in the hospitals needed their clean laundry. Rain or shine, hot or cold, our family did whatever it took to get the job done. It was an issue of serving and doing what we said we would do. Dad called it integrity.

Sometimes it meant pulling through even when it was tough. Dad taught us to do whatever we did with all our heart. He believed in serving the customer, being honest, taking responsibility. A job half done didn't cut it with my dad. It didn't represent adequately either his business or the Rosberg name.

There was another dad who challenged his son to be the best he could be. Listen to these words from King David:

> And you, my son Solomon, acknowledge the God of your father,
> and serve him with wholehearted devotion and with a willing
> mind, for the Lord searches every heart and understands every

motive behind the thoughts. If you seek him, he will be found by you; but if you forsake him, he will reject you forever. (1 Chronicles 28:9)

Nothing can be hidden from God. He knows your heart. He knows whether you serve Him as a man after God's own heart. He also knows if self-ishness has crept in and taken control of your heart.

So if God is always watching, and if working wholeheartedly is His command and His design, how does work become a threat? Why do so many men get tripped up and lose the proper perspective of a healthy balance between work and their homes?

Sometimes it's because we don't respond to danger signs.

The Danger

Traveling down Interstate 80 recently, I saw flashing lights ahead. Barricades crisscrossed the road, giving ample warning of road construction. As I approached the site, I saw men and women who were working hard under the heat of the summer sun while thousands of cars passed by each day.

Drivers had been warned to slow down and be alert. Nevertheless some cars were whizzing by too fast, endangering the safety both of workers and of other motorists. Some of the lane-marking cones meant to steer cars away from equipment and the workers had been knocked aside.

All the elements of danger were present: high rates of speed, workers vulnerable to the elements, pressures to get the job done on time, excessive traffic.

Sounds like our careers, doesn't it? We move quickly at high speeds, trying to do more and more with less and less time, money, and manpower. Workers are vulnerable to all sorts of elements: office politics, downsizing, sexual tempta-tion, lack of training, excessive competition. Are there pressures to get the job done on time? Yes, probably like you experienced just yesterday or today. And how about the excessive traffic? If you live and work like I do, you face that one every day. The demands of phone calls, budgets, project deadlines, personality clashes, contradictory goals, you name it. Our worksites need danger signs as much as I-80 does.

Here's the scoop. For most of us, our work in and of itself is not dangerous. But work *out of balance* is dangerous both to our health and the health of our family.

Of course we need to work. "If anyone does not provide for his relatives and especially for his immediate family," Paul said, "he has denied the faith and is worse than an unbeliever" (1 Timothy 5:8). It couldn't be much clearer. If we don't provide for our families, we're in deep weeds. God calls us to provide. It's our role to provide material provision for our families.

What does that mean? For some it's a roof over our heads, food, adequate clothing. For others it's Air Jordan sneakers, trips to Disneyland during spring break, designer clothes, the works. This chapter isn't designed to answer the question of "how much provision is enough?" But it is designed to ask you as a man this question: "Are you so stuck on *material* provision that you are failing to give the *emotional* provision your wife and kids need?"

Emotional provision means not only that the lights are on, but also that someone is home. It means that in addition to providing materially, you save enough energy to invest in the personal needs of your family. It means being generous with your time, your affection, your wisdom, your companionship. It doesn't mean you don't work hard. It means you save enough of *you* to connect heart-to-heart. The job isn't done when you've brought home a paycheck, no matter how big it is.

Balance

God created us to work, but that work must be in balance. Maybe you have it in balance. You're fulfilled in your job, but that isn't the be-all and end-all of your existence. You have a proper perspective, knowing that someone was doing the job before you and someone will pick it up when you leave. You may be quite creative and successful, but your identity isn't defined solely by the marketplace.

Or perhaps you're realizing that this area of life is out of balance. You may be working two jobs to make ends meet. You may be doing yeoman's labor just to provide for your family. Or maybe work is out of balance for you because it's the only place you're fulfilled. You do your job well, and going home brings only the stress of a fragmented family. You find yourself staying at the office a few more hours or nights than ever before, and you sense your family slipping from you.

Or maybe you're squarely in denial. I once saw a T-shirt that said, "Denial. It isn't a river in Egypt." Everyone—from your wife and kids and parents to the family dog—knows your work schedule is out of balance. Everyone, that is, but you. You may have been told, but you haven't listened. You've closed off any input because down deep, you're afraid to hear the truth. And until a crisis hits, you're likely to continue the pattern.

Balance in your work life doesn't mean you don't work extra hours from time to time. We all do that. It doesn't mean you don't "go for it" and be the best you can be in your career. We all want to pursue excellence. What balance means is that you ask yourself the hard questions, and you're willing to listen to those who know and love you.

When you come home night after night so exhausted that you have nothing left for your family, you ask yourself if you're into a destructive pattern. When your kids stop talking to you about school, problems, or fun times, you ask yourself if you may be out of balance. When you've missed the family dinner three nights this week, and can't remember the last time you saw your son play ball, and can't remember the instrument your daughter plays, you ask yourself whether you've crossed the line.

Balance isn't a trap, but a protection—God's protection—so that we win in our homes and cross the finish line with our wives and kids.

These are hard times for men. We're being pulled both ways. On one hand we're trying to keep balance so we can succeed as husbands and dads. On the other hand, the marketplace where we're trying to survive is getting more and more competitive. Many companies are downsizing. Many men are losing their jobs, and countless others are anxious about losing theirs. Many who do manage to keep steady work are faced with a smaller paycheck. We're all being asked to do more with less in our businesses, and we feel the crunch. It all adds up to unwanted pressure for men committed to guarding their hearts in the marketplace.

Our families and our culture demand that we find the balance. If we don't, we're going to lose our families. You can always get another job, but replacing your family is something else again.

Our work has its own built-in tension, being designed as it is to meet our own needs as well as the needs of our families, our employers, and our Lord. Maybe you sense these needs pushing at you from all sides, leaving you in a major crunch. If you feel that stress, take a look at these three plumb lines.

- First, is your work *pleasing to God?* Not only the actual work, but the way you work—your motivation, your use of time, your attitudes toward the job. If you believe that what you're doing is pleasing to God, then you're on the right track.

- Second, ask yourself, "Is my family consistently getting only the leftovers of my mental and emotional energy because of my excessive work? Am I offering too little emotional provision at home?" We all have episodes of work stress. That isn't the problem. But if there is a *pattern* to it, we need to take a long, hard look at the impact our work is having on our family.

- Third, is your work pushing you into the danger zone regarding your own emotional, mental, and physical health? If so, it would be wise to get a personal checkup to inventory your work patterns and make some adjustments. Analyze how your emotional strength, mental strength, and physical strength are typically expended, and how (and if) you're replenishing yourself in each of those areas.

An Investment Analysis

One evening, over a plateful of blackened redfish, my friend Dennis Rainey challenged me to count the cost of my own overburdened schedule. As we were discussing the ministries God had allowed me to be involved in, Dennis put down his fork and said, "Gary, God has given you many arenas of effectiveness for Him: counseling, speaking, writing, and men's ministry—to name a few.

You have the potential to enjoy success in any of those areas. But if you aren't careful, you'll spread yourself too thin and become ineffective in your calling—as well as in your home.

"The question you need to ask yourself is not where *can* you succeed, but where *must* you succeed? Tell me something, Gary. If you put all the energy you put into your ministry in one hand, and the energy and focus you put into your home in the other hand, what would happen if you flip-flopped them? What would happen to your ministry? What would happen to your home?"

Wise questions from a wise man. In fact, I didn't finish my dinner. You see, out of his love for me, he challenged me to strike the balance. My family demands I find the balance. So does yours, friend.

And if the balance is at times lost as you tip one way or the other, let it tip in the direction of home and family rather than career. If you *must* choose between climbing the career ladder or "being there" for your wife and kids—which side do you honestly want to win? Ask yourself: Isn't it better—much better, in heaven's economy—for your job and career to suffer than for your family to suffer?

Fortune or Family?

So how do we do win at home? How do we guard our hearts so that we find the balance and stay out of the danger zone?

Let's go back to the Bible. Jesus said,

> What good is it for a man to gain the whole world, and yet lose or forfeit his very self? (Luke 9:25)

He could just have easily asked, "What good is it for a man to gain the whole world, and yet lose or forfeit his own family?"

I don't want to sacrifice my family at the altar of the job. I almost did that in 1983 when my daughter left me out of the family picture. She was the only one who managed to get my attention. My pastor, wife, parents, and friends all tried, to no avail. But Sarah's picture changed my life.

Still, it took *two years* to pull away from the excessive work patterns and get back to the place God most wants me to win: in the home. He wants me to provide not only financially, but also (and more importantly) emotionally and spiritually for the needs of my wife and kids. And He wants you to do the same.

A few generations ago, a man captured the essence of this truth in some powerful words about the balance between home and career. When I read this good counsel written by Edgar Guest in *My Job as a Father* back in 1923, I can almost see the ghost of Solomon in the background, sadly nodding his head.

Read it and take heed. Guest wrote:

> I have known of a number of wealthy men who were not successes as fathers. They made money rapidly; their factories were marvels of organization; their money investments were sound and made with excellent judgment, and their contributions to public service were useful and willingly made. All this took time and thought. At the finish there was a fortune on the one hand, and a worthless and dissolute son on the other. WHY? Too much time spent in making money implies too little time spent with the boy.
>
> When these children were youngsters romping on the floor, if someone had come to any one of those fathers and offered him a million dollars for his lad he would have spurned the offer and kicked the proposer out of doors. Had someone offered him ten million dollars in cash for the privilege of making a drunkard out of his son, the answer would have been the same. Had someone offered to buy from him for a fortune the privilege of playing with the boy, of going on picnics and fishing trips and outings, and being with him a part of every day, he would have refused the proposition without giving it a second thought.
>
> Yet that is exactly the bargain those men made, and which many men are still making. They are coining their lives into fortunes and automobile factories and great industries, but their boys are growing up as they may. These men probably will succeed in business; but they will be failures as fathers. To me it seems that a little less industry and a little more comradeship with the boy is more desirable.
>
> Not so much of me in the bank, and more of me and of my best in the lad, is what I should like to have to show at the end of my career.

> To be the father of a great son is what I should call
> success…This is what I conceive my job to be.

I'll tell you honestly, there's nothing I want more than to succeed at home. It's a desire I hear reverberating in the following poem, also written by Edgar Guest.

> I must be fit for a child to follow,
> scorning the places where loose men wallow;
> knowing how much he shall learn from me,
> I must be fair as I'd have him be.
> I must come home to him day by day,
> clean as the morning I went away.
> I must be fit for a child's glad greeting;
> his are eyes that there is no cheating.
> He must behold me in every test,
> not at my worst but my very best;
> he must be proud when my life is done
> to have men know that he is my son.

I never met Mr. Guest or his son. But my guess is that the legacy passed on from father to son is being passed on today to his grandchildren and great-grandchildren. Guest challenged his son not only in his words but in his example. His wisdom is timeless. He knew the perils of men who sold out to the ever mighty dollar instead of building the character of the children God has given to us.

Work Is Not the Problem

Listen to the following words from another letter I received from a man who attended a marriage conference:

> Sunday morning you quoted a book I had just finished, *Confessions of an Ad Man* by David Ogilvy. The quote was along the lines of "if you're a good father and spend time with your family, I'll probably like you better, but don't cry to me when it comes time for a raise or a promotion." When I read the book I thought, *Yeah, that makes sense, I better really buckle down and work harder.* When you read that passage in the context of family commitment, I felt

as though I had been hit in the stomach. How is it possible that I had my values and priorities so screwed up?

Work isn't our problem. Our hearts are. And if we are trying to fill some clawing need in our hearts by excessive work—rather than investing in our relationships at home—then we all lose.

We were designed to work by a Father who also knows our every need. He understands the tension in our lives and hearts. He understands the insecurities we carry, wondering if we are ever able to do enough with our kids. He understands, like no other, the love of a Father for a son. In love He gave up His Son so we could live. But to give up His Son, it took a reason as big as the loving salvation of mankind. He doesn't want me to give up my children for the sake of a mere career.

We were designed to work, and our work is good and honorable. We need to do our best and to give our employers their money's worth. We need to be wholehearted men in whatever we do, both on the job and at home. That may mean you won't get promoted as fast on the job. It may mean you won't make as much money. It may mean there won't be as many bonuses or perks.

But it will probably also mean that your wife and kids will finish the race with you. And nothing can compare to that!

Guard your heart.

Application Suggestions:

1. Name the three people who probably observe your work most closely, and who have the most acquaintance with your work habits. How do you think each one would describe your work? At an appropriate time and setting, ask at least one of them to give you a candid evaluation of your work habits.

2. Deeply consider your own "track record" in working wholeheartedly and for the Lord, according to the guidelines in Colossians 3:23-24. How would you express (in a prayer to God) your own commitment to working at your job in this way?

3. Make a list (as complete as possible) of *all* your work motivations—*why* do you work? Then rank them in order of importance.

4. On the same sheet of paper, make a note of the circumstances in which it is easiest for you to get "out of balance" in the area of work—when you spend too much time and energy at it, to the neglect of your family. When this happens, which of the work motivations you listed is pushing you the hardest? (Place a check by it.)

5. State briefly what you believe to be the minimum adequate level of material provision for *your* family at this time. You could express it in terms of a yearly income figure, or perhaps in a list of the actual physical necessities your family requires. Give yourself a grade—A, B, C, D, or F —on how well you consistently come through with this provision.

6. Now state briefly in your own words what you believe to be the minimum adequate level of *emotional* provision for your family. Again, the choice of terms is up to you. And once more, give yourself a grade for how consistently you come through with this provision.

To Think About & Discuss:

1. Look again at Colossians 3:22-24. What perspective do these verses bring to your daily work? In what ways does knowing your primary responsibility to please the Lord Jesus actually increase your work responsibility? How might it also release you from stress and pressure?

2. Quoting 1 Thessalonians 4:11-12, the author shows that the integrity and quality of our work has a direct bearing on the effectiveness of our witness to outsiders. Review these verses and describe how they could apply to your own work and career this week.

CHAPTER SIX

FRONTAL ATTACK #2:
DISTRACTIONS

■

Distractions. We all have them.

In moments of encouragement and vision we set goals for our growth in Christ, for our families, for our work. But the moments of encouragement and vision are followed by weeks and months of daily grind and hourly interruptions. The goals get blurred or buried.

We sit down on Sunday afternoon and make our list of "should do's, would like to do's, and must do's" for the week ahead. But by Monday afternoon we've been thrown so many curves that we toss the list and call for a time out.

I wonder...what's distracting you?

- Is it pleasure you live for—the weekend, the good times, fun and comfort, R & R?
- Is it power you're seeking—the power you think you need to make the difference you want to make, to make things happen the way you want them to happen?
- Is it the bucks? Are you under the illusion that getting into the next pay grade, making that big sale, or winning that lotto will make all of your problems go away?
- Is it striving for some position? To be high-profile, to be *somebody* and everybody knows it?

Don't dismiss these distractions too quickly. Think about them: pleasure, power, money, position. Here are things that guys all over the country have told me are blinding them.

And they're the same things that plagued the "king of distractions."

King of Distractions

Like the typical man today, King Solomon was searching for what would fill his life and bring true satisfaction. Unlike the typical man today, Solomon was able to indulge himself in anything and everything in his attempt to find fulfillment. Listen to the voice of experience (and regret) in Ecclesiastes 2.

> I thought in my heart, "Come now, I will test you with pleasure to find out what is good." But that also proved to be meaningless. "Laughter," I said, "is foolish. And what does pleasure accomplish?" I tried cheering myself with wine, and embracing folly—my mind still guiding me with wisdom. I wanted to see what was worthwhile for men to do under heaven during the few days of their lives.
>
> I undertook great projects: I built houses for myself and planted vineyards. I made gardens and parks and planted all kinds of fruit trees in them. I made reservoirs to water groves of flourishing trees. I bought male and female slaves and had other slaves who were born in my house. I also owned more herds and flocks than anyone in Jerusalem before me. I amassed silver and gold for myself, and the treasure of kings and provinces. I acquired men and women singers, and a harem as well—the delights of the heart of man, I became greater by far than anyone in Jerusalem before me....

Pleasure. Power. Money. Position. Solomon had it all. In his pursuit to please his aching soul, he lived beyond the brink. He sought out any pleasure he could find.

> I denied myself nothing my eyes desired; I refused my heart no pleasure. My heart took delight in all my work, and this was the reward for all my labor.

And his conclusion?

> Yet when I surveyed all that my hands had done and what I had
> toiled to achieve, everything was meaningless, a chasing after the
> wind; nothing was gained under the sun.

He doesn't say, "I didn't gain much." He doesn't say, "I could have gained more if I struck a balance."

What Solomon says is, "NOTHING WAS GAINED."

Nothing.

Can you imagine one of today's kingpins concluding that all of his empire was meaningless and empty? That in reality he possessed nothing at all?

Solomon has discovered truths that most men never realize. Truly a man of wisdom, he has learned from what he has seen, though the lessons were hurtful. Can you hear the pain in his writing? He is broken.

But he's not done. He has learned to see distraction even in the pursuit of human wisdom:

> Then I turned my thoughts to consider wisdom, and also madness
> and folly. What more can the king's successor do than what has
> already been done? I saw that wisdom is better than folly, just as
> light is better than darkness. The wise man has eyes in his head,
> while the fool walks in the darkness; but I came to realize that the
> same fate overtakes them both.
>
> Then I thought in my heart...

Before we go on, notice the punch line: "THEN I THOUGHT IN MY HEART..."

His *heart*. Not his head. Solomon hadn't forgotten that the heart is the wellspring. After listing the pain of his varied endeavors, the worthlessness of his many accomplishments, he comes out here: It all goes back to the heart.

And what's true for Solomon is true for you and me: Our heart is the wellspring of life, the source from where it all flows. The real truth of your motives, your attitudes, your beliefs, your soul, is revealed with an inside look at your heart.

Back to Solomon:

> Then I thought in my heart, "The fate of the fool will overtake me
> also. What then do I gain by being wise?" I said in my heart, "This
> too is meaningless."

Let's look more closely at the distractions that Solomon—and men today —have known well.

Pleasure

After a long day or a long week at work, there's nothing better than kicking off the shoes, putting on some loose gym shorts, grabbing a Diet Coke and popcorn, parking in your favorite chair in front of the TV, and turning on the game. Quite frankly, you've earned it (at least that's what you tell yourself). Just sitting there. Just relaxing. It feels so good.

Or maybe your pleasure is more active. We all like to play, whether it's picking up some clubs and hitting the little white ball, a furious game of racquetball, or heading down to the nets for tennis. And then there's the joy of hunting and dropping a line in your favorite river or fishing hole. Or heading down to the speedway or to a wrestling meet.

From working on cars to screaming at the ump at the baseball park, we're all the same. We like our pleasure. And there's nothing wrong with it—as long as it stays in balance.

Pleasure within boundaries is good. It's when it spills out of boundaries that it becomes a distraction, and at times a fatal distraction. Fatal to our time with God, fatal to our wife and kids, fatal to our physical well-being.

Solomon failed to keep his pleasures in balance and it eventually destroyed his nation. You're probably not a king, but let me ask you: Are your pleasures in balance? When it comes to your discretionary time, does hunting, fishing, golf, or TV sports get only a piece of your action...or most of it? Do your wife and kids get only the leftovers? Is your motto "Work Hard, Play Hard, Family Hardly At All"?

It's not wrong to go after pleasure. Just make sure you seek it with balance. If you don't know what that balance is, ask your wife and kids. They'll help you fill in the blanks.

And ask God too. Have you tried looking at your pleasure from His point of view? What does it mean to "do" pleasure His way? Take some cues from Solomon's dad—David, the man after God's own heart. Ask yourself what

David meant when he told God, "You fill me with joy in your presence, with eternal *pleasures* at your right hand" (Psalm 16:11), and when he told us, *"Delight* yourself in the Lord and he will give you the *desires* of your heart" (37:4). Is it easy for you to agree with David that God is a God *"who satisfies your desires with good things"* (103:5)? When it comes down to it, your Father in heaven wants you to find pleasure even more than you do. He'll also provide that pleasure—real pleasure that truly satisfies.

Pleasure is not the problem. It's your *heart* toward pleasure that matters.

Power

We men have been jockeying for power since we were little boys pushing and shoving our way to be first and get the most and have the best. An insatiable desire for power doesn't have to be taught, it comes natural. We're selfish, and power opens the door to indulge that selfishness.

Our culture has a lasting love affair with power. Left and right we find seminars, books, magazines, and messages telling us how to get power and keep it. You'll find your appetite for power amply whetted by the latest titles on the bookstore shelves:

Awakening the Giant Within

Close any Deal

Swimming with Sharks

Both our selfishness and our culture perpetuate our quest for power. When we strive constantly to gain more power, we can be sure that we're the victims of distraction and distortion.

And yet, *having* power isn't really the problem. The problem comes either in *pursuing* it, or *misusing* it.

So how do we approach power in a healthy way?

The answer is that we submit it to God. We allow God to be the only source of our power, and the only governor of it.

Listen again to David: "It is God who arms me with *strength"* (Psalm 18:32). "The Lord is the *stronghold* of my life" (27:1). "The God of Israel gives *power* and *strength* to his people" (68:35).

As with pleasure, so with power—God will give you the right kind, in the right way, and in the right timing, and for the right purposes. If you really believe that, you won't get distracted by seeking power or using it wrongly.

Power is not the problem. It's your *heart* toward power that matters.

Money

Remember the lines the Beatles sang? "Can't buy me love, can't buy me love… money can't buy me love." Takes me back to the sixties. Back then it was just a song. But it's more than a song. It is truth, a truth Solomon learned late.

He purchased and possessed to an extreme. "I amassed silver and gold for myself," he says, "and the treasure of kings and provinces."

Of course, God Himself is the One who made Solomon wealthy, just as He had promised to do (1 Kings 3:13). So money itself is not the problem. What matters is our heart attitude toward getting, having, and using the money.

How much is enough? Too often our answer is a perpetual "just a little more." It's good to ask yourself, "How much should I accumulate?" But even more important is to ask, "How am I accumulating it, and why?" I'm all for setting financial goals and going for it. But not at the cost of relationships— with God, with family, and with others. And not outside the much larger goals of what God has called and equipped and gifted us for. Don't allow money to blur your vision of what God is doing in your life.

God has as much to say in His Word about money and wealth and buying and possessing as He does about almost anything. We have plenty of guidelines in Scripture for doing what's right when it comes to money.

Maybe the best guideline to start with is what Jesus said in Luke 16:13— "You cannot serve both God and Money." Money's a great servant, but the worst possible master.

I know men who are possessed by money. Some dollar figure got stuck in their minds—so many hundred thousand or million—and they've decided there's no worth, security, or meaning in life until they achieve that golden number. So they work like dogs, distracted by the accumulation of money, and completely miss out on real life.

But you don't need a specific amount in mind to be consumed by the pursuit of money, and you don't even have to be accumulating it in order to live as if you were. As someone has said, our debt-ridden society is addicted to "spending money we don't have on things we don't need to keep up with people we don't know."

Most men my age and older have parents who endured the Great Depression, and who earned every penny of their money. But nearly everyone in my generation has experienced the "good life" and has never done without. How will we handle the nation's wealth that is being passed on to us? Probably the same way we handle it in our own homes today: Many spend every cent they have (plus some) and grow desperate, while only a few are good stewards.

It's our job to take care of our family's physical needs, and money makes that possible. So earn all you need, earn it well, and be good stewards of it. Just don't be blinded by it.

Position

Climbing to the next rung on the corporate ladder, reaching that big office, being chosen to lead a church committee or a community club—it all seems to scream "worthiness."

But the dreaming and the seeking and the striving and the jockeying for these positions are, to quote Solomon, like "chasing after the wind" (Ecclesiastes 2:11). Eventually, and maybe quite soon, these positions we drove to achieve will belong to someone else. In most of these situations, if we died tonight, by eight o'clock tomorrow morning a perfectly adequate replacement would be ready to go. Positions come and go.

You may be very good in the various positions you hold. Whatever the role, you may excel in it. Solomon certainly did. "I became greater *by far* than anyone in Jerusalem before me," he wrote (2:9). He was king of Israel at the height of his nation's territorial expansion and prosperity. He had reached the top of the top. He was great, even greater than his father. But turn over several pages in Scripture and we read, "Someone greater than Solomon is here" (Matthew 12:42).

Whatever job you hold, you may be better by far than anyone before you —the best salesman in your company, the best carpenter or plumber in your community, the best attorney or physician in your practice, the best technician in your lab, the best teacher in your school. But more than likely, some young buck is in training right now to move in and do even better.

But in your own home, no one will ever be as perfectly designed and equipped as you are for your God-appointed role as husband to your wife and dad to your kids. I often say that Barbara and the girls don't need some other knucklehead to come in and lead the family. They already have a knucklehead —me. And I intend to stick around and finish the job God gave me.

How Much Damage?

Distractions. Have you identified any that injure you and your family? Let me tell you about one that almost did me in.

A few years ago I was writing my first book, *Choosing to Love Again*. I spent most of my time writing in my basement study. I wrote on weekends and in the early mornings. There were times on those weekday mornings when my kids would come downstairs on their way to school to say goodbye, but I would be so engrossed in writing that I wouldn't respond to them.

When the book was finished, I learned from Barbara that I had lost some of the connectedness with Missy that we both needed. Soon afterward I was invited to speak at a conference in Orlando, and I agreed with one stipulation: that Missy could join me. They needed a speaker and Missy needed her dad.

We boarded the plane with a little wall between us. As I wrapped up the conference, we headed off for a few days in the Magic Kingdom and on the beach. During one of my braver moments I asked a difficult question: "Missy, how much damage did I do to our relationship by writing this book?"

"Dad," she said, "I don't want to get sad-spirited tonight."

Ouch. A direct hit from one of the most precious people in my life!

"I know honey," I replied, "but sometimes we need to be sad-spirited if it leads to sharing our hearts."

So she opened up. "The hardest thing, Dad, was when I would sometimes come downstairs before school to tell you something and you would say, 'Just a minute, honey, let me finish this thought on the computer.' Sometimes I would wait and you would never look back up. So I would just go off to school."

Distractions. By the grace of God, once again, through the open, vulnerable heart of a resilient and wonderful young lady, a father learned a life-changing message.

We closed the loop after lots of talks during those few days. We laughed, we played, we stayed up late, we had ice cream, we rode rides, we walked the beach hand in hand picking up seashells. When we returned home on a cold, Iowa winter day and walked off the airplane, Barb said she could see the sparkle back in Missy's eyes. We were together, and we were home.

Distractions. They get in the way, and meanwhile time slips through your hands. Suddenly you've raised your kids and they're gone. And the questions race through your mind: How did they grow up so fast? Where has the time gone? What have I missed?

Distractions. You're absorbed in them, and you're running hard. Meanwhile your wife stops asking you for date nights and begins filling her needs with other things, other people, other visions.

Distractions can be fatal, my friend. Go home and guard your family. Solomon didn't, and it cost him his heart, his nation, and his family. You want proof? Listen to the scriptural epitaph applied to Solomon's son, Rehoboam, who followed in his father's footsteps: "He did evil because he had not set his heart on seeking the Lord" (2 Chronicles 12:14). Solomon allowed himself to be distracted by pleasure, power, money, and position. And it cost him his son.

So guard your heart, beware of distractions. Seek God.

No other choice is worth making.

Application Suggestions:

1. Put the four headings "Pleasure," "Power," "Money," and "Position" across the top of a sheet of paper. Then spend some time thinking back over your life for the past three years. What have been the most significant distractions facing you during that time? List them under the appropriate category.

2. On that same sheet of paper, circle the heading which seems to represent the most consistent area of distraction for you. Analyze the reasons for this pattern. What does this tell you about yourself?

3. Show this sheet of paper to your wife, and explain to her what you were doing. Then ask for her comments and insight.

4. Think again about the principles outlined in Philippians 4:6-7 — how God's *peace* guards your heart and mind in Christ, and how that peace comes when you pray thoroughly and thankfully about everything (instead of worrying). Write out a prayer to God that sincerely expresses your desire for His help in overcoming the *distractions* you face in life.

To Think About & Discuss:

1. In his section about the distraction of money, the author quotes Luke 16:13 and adds, "Money is a great servant, but the worst possible master." How could money move from a position of servant in our lives to the position of master? How can we make it serve us once again, after allowing it to rule our lives?

2. Read Ecclesiastes 2:11. How is an endless "jockeying for position" in our life and career like "chasing after wind"?

3. Take time to read and consider a slice of Paul's heart in Philippians 3:7-14, considering especially verses 13-14. Describe the apostle's single-minded approach to life. How did this approach keep him from life-sapping, energy-draining distractions?

4. The author suggests we consider Psalms 16:11, 37:4, and 103:5 as a correction to out-of-balance pleasure seeking. What wisdom do these verses bring to the pursuit of recreation and pleasure?

CHAPTER SEVEN

·····································

FRONTAL ATTACK #3:

RELATIONSHIP PRESSURES

■

Have you ever been in crossfire? What does that word bring to mind?

Maybe you're a veteran of a war zone. You fought in the Persian Gulf or Vietnam or Korea. You know what real crossfire is all about. Your life depended on how you responded to it.

Or perhaps you recall a many-sided family argument: a time of too many people letting too many words fly, filling a home with hurt and regret.

Or maybe what comes to mind is an unforgettable snowball fight. You packed your ammunition cold and tight as ice, and gave it a fling. So did "the enemy." You gave a grin for each hit you scored, and a grimace of pain whenever you were successfully targeted.

All crossfire situations have a lot in common: You don't know which direction the next shot is coming from, you often feel out of control, and (unless it's all in fun) you want out QUICK!

The Real Thing

Patrolman Paul Bennett and his partner hit the streets for their three-to-eleven shift—on Paul's ninth day without a break. It was hot and humid. Summer time in the big city. The heat index was soaring and the mood on the streets was boiling over. Crime had spread from back alleys and crack houses to neighborhoods that were once safe for families. People were running scared, and they were frustrated. Tempers were flaring. All police vacations were canceled.

The "good guys" at the station were showing the effects of the stress. Morale around the precinct was as out-of-whack as the spinal x-rays of a fifty-five-year-old retired defensive tackle.

Paul felt more than ever like walking away from it all. He had sixteen years to go to get his pension, but each day seemed like an eternity. He was wearing down.

Tensions were high even in Paul Bennett's family. It didn't make sense. In fact, not much of anything made sense anymore in Paul's turbulent city or in his life. He was living in the midst of crossfire, both on the job and at home.

His once solid marriage was in the ninth inning, his kids didn't reach out to him much anymore, and the credit card companies were calling day and night. Paul was popping antacids left and right, and waking up with the sweats every night.

On that hot afternoon of Paul's ninth straight workday, he and his partner, Frank, were called to quell what they thought was a family conflict. What Paul didn't know as they responded to that 10-16 code (domestic disturbance) was that it would be the last trip he would make with Frank after twelve years of working together. A simple family feud would turn into crossfire that brought an end to their partnership.

Stepping onto the front porch, the two officers heard screaming coming from inside the house. But it wasn't just the voice of a couple having a Friday night argument. There were other voices. Paul and Frank paused briefly to listen.

Turning to each other, they quickly realized they were up against more than a husband and wife having it out. They had happened on a drug deal in progress.

Suddenly the door opened. As Paul pulled back, he saw Frank take a bullet in the shoulder. Both men went different directions on the porch, trying to take cover. Paul found protection, but his partner was still exposed.

Things soon went from bad to worse. A second shooter from the upstairs window began firing.

Scrambling to the side of the house, Paul watched helplessly as his partner was under attack from two different directions. Crossfire.

Paul radioed for backup. "Officer down. 125 Elm Street. Request immediate assistance."

Frank was finally able to position himself behind an oak tree in the front yard, but could get no further. Now gunfire had started from another window on the first story.

The sound of shooting was soon mixed with the wail of sirens. Within the next several minutes, the neighborhood looked like a war zone. Officers and a SWAT team surrounded the house.

Paul and Frank were still pinned down, and the extent of Frank's injuries were unknown.

Paul stood almost frozen under the spray of bullets. His eyes moved rapidly from Frank, to the windows of the house, to the team of officers trying desperately to seize the gunmen.

An hour later, it was over. Frank was taken away in an ambulance. He would be permanently disabled.

As Paul was driven away in the squad car he and Frank had shared, he felt ready to go over the edge in despair and loss. The crossfire had taken out one officer and left another in emotional shambles.

Taking Apart Men's Hearts

The word *crossfire* is defined as "the firing of guns from two or more points so that the lines of fire cross." Whether on violent city streets or in the living rooms of homes on the brink, men's hearts are the enemy's purposeful target, and he sends his fire from as many directions as possible. When men today are under crossfire, getting hit from several directions at once, almost always the assault from at least one direction involves a relationship in crisis. Many times there seem to be several relationships in crisis all at the same time.

You've been there. I call it relational crossfire. We feel pummeled. It leaves us spinning like a top.

- Your wife is reaching out but you can't get past the anger and frustration still brewing from the last blowup. You're stressed beyond the max and haven't got the map on how to repair the hurts you both feel. What was once a fun loving marriage has turned to a distant relationship.

- Your kids have gone from toddlerhood to teendom, and nothing is like it used to be. They're over the boundary but you don't have the juice to draw the line. Your wife keeps asking you to take the lead and support her, but you find yourself pulling away.

- Your parents are increasingly needy and dependent. They're asking for more and more from you, and you feel you have less to give than ever. You just don't know how to parent a mom and dad who have always been so solid and capable. It's downright scary.

- A friend and coworker is charging up the ladder, leaving you behind. In the aftermath, he's pushing buttons inside you that you really wish weren't part of your makeup, but they are. All the trust has been drained from your friendship, replaced by resentment and a sense of being betrayed.

These kind of bullets can rip hearts wide open. Everywhere you turn you seem to encounter stress, emotion, demands, pressure. You're blowing up more frequently followed by shutting down and withdrawing.

Been there? I have. And like you, I will be again.

Maybe you're on the way there now. If so, let me ask you another question: Do you want to pull out of this tailspin before it takes you down? Let me give you a map that could help you deal with the stress and pressure of relational crossfire. You don't have to tube out in these situations.

We need just three things: a plan, the reminder that the Lord will carry us, and the courage to take the steps to guard our hearts and finish the race well.

My Days on the Front Line

I once went through a week of crossfire that I'd like to forget, but my memory bank won't let me. It was too valuable in the character-building department to let go of. It was a time that I not-so-fondly remember as "hell week."

Three crisis situations at my counseling office that week in mid-December put an already overcharged schedule into hyperdrive. The first involved a well-respected pastor who had just joined the painful list of church leaders guilty of adultery. He had broken the hearts of hundreds who felt betrayed by the man who had pastored their church for years.

Later that week, a teenage girl had threatened suicide. She was placed in a local mental health unit, leaving her family in a turmoil of emotions.

Then came jarring news from another family whom I had been counseling with all my heart and soul. The mother in that family left home in the middle of the night without leaving a trace of where she was headed. It would be nine days before we heard from her. (She would say that she had hit the wall and could no longer see any hope. A cheap motel had become her sanctuary.) She left a husband and three children in shock. The death of a family.

I felt caught under a spray of bullets.

Barb and I were trying to keep our heads above water in the midst of the pressure. Our weekly date nights and evening talks, the very life blood of our marriage, were getting pushed to the side in order to meet the demands on every front of ministry and relationships. We were battle weary and a little frayed on the nerve endings. Pink phone message slips were piling up and I hadn't paid bills in over a month.

Then the crossfire began to get much closer to home. My mom phoned to say my dad was struggling with some health issues that needed immediate attention.

Then Barb called me at the office.

"Gary," she said with a strangely tense voice, "it's Missy."

Lord, I instinctively prayed, *anything but my kids. Please not them!*

"Gary, we have to get her to the hospital. She isn't shaking this virus the way we thought she would."

Those tempered words still ring in my ears. Words from my wife, my lifelong partner, who was as scared under the surface as I was. It was as if we were both faking a calm response, knowing we had to rise to the occasion. This was no time to panic, at least on the outside.

Our three-year-old Missy had gone through appointment after appointment by good doctors, and had taken enough pills to stock a pharmacy. But nothing had checked the wild virus that was charging through her body. Now her physician wanted to hospitalize her.

Barb and I were both relieved to know Missy would have the top-notch care she needed, but we were also feeling pretty vulnerable.

Here it was, six days before Christmas. It was clear the Rosbergs' holiday would have an entirely different spin on it this year. We didn't even have a Christmas tree yet, and the festive spirit that typically filled our home in that season had to yield to something far more important.

We would now be sitting day and night in a children's hospital watching Missy fight the virus with all her heart. The serious illness of a loved one sure puts the rest of life in perspective, doesn't it? Whether the bills get paid, the oil changed, or the phone calls returned really don't matter much when a little daughter lies in a hospital bed.

How do you think I handled that week? I wish I could say with grace and patient endurance. But that isn't true. In fact I got shook. Real shook.

My response went through three stages. At first I held everything in, stuffing the emotions that were being stoked like a flaming furnace.

Later, in a very safe moment with Barb, I expressed some of those emotions and fears that were eating a hole in my heart. If felt strange to do that—being a man and all—but it helped me process what I was experiencing, and it drew us closer together.

Finally, I did what you would have done. I rose to the call, and headed bravely into the storm doing my best in a seemingly impossible set of circumstances.

But just when my emotions got back in order, my body crashed. With fatigue and stress at an all time high, my lower back began to go out, I couldn't sleep, and my heart felt as if it would leap out of my chest.

I remember sitting on the edge of my bed while all those pressures swirled in my head. *How am I ever going to get through all of this?*

To be honest with you, I was scared. The work stuff was hard enough. When you're in a position of helping other people, sometimes you look in the mirror and feel so stinking inadequate you don't know what to do. So you pray for God's wisdom and do the best you can. I knew enough to do that again.

As for the bills and phone messages, I knew they would get tended to in (somewhat) due time.

But when I thought about my dad and his health problems, I really began to feel the stress. I began asking myself questions that sent chills down my spine: *How long do I have with him, God? How can I best encourage him? How can I be everything I want to be to make our good relationship even better? Have I told him everything he means to me? Are there any regrets?*

As I sat at Missy's bedside, watching her labored breathing, and seeing Barb sitting there with all the love and protection a mother can have, I knew God had a plan in this whole thing. In the midst of the raging waters I was blind to it. But eventually, as things began to slow down, I would see how He was bringing us closer together.

It took time. It took getting on the back side of that week—that week of crossfire when the enemy was loaded for bear—before I could begin to see what God was doing.

Not If, But When

If you're anything like me, you live in a pressure cooker much of the time. The stage of life you're in is full of stress: Your family is growing, your career is developing, your marriage is changing, and your parents are aging. You have a wife to love and lead, kids to be a dad to, and parents to care for in their golden years.

Each of these relationships is a privilege, but each is also a priority that includes some stress.

We have relationship pressures. And there'll be times when these pressures converge—when you're caught in the crossfire and the enemy has you in his crosshairs. It will happen. It's not *if,* but *when.*

Sometimes the pressures will combine high intensity, high frequency, and long duration, and they become especially threatening. Something has to give in these times. Pressure is pressure, and when it hits, it has to come out somewhere. You've been there. So have I. And will you be there again? Yep. And me too.

So the question is, *When* these pressures hit, what will we do? Will we fold? Or will we step into the eye of the storm and take it on with the help of our gracious and loving God?

I can tell you what I usually do: I sweat. I get shook for a time. Then sometimes I try to shove it down and tough it out. I'm still learning.

So let's get at the meat of this thing and look at three basic principles for guarding our hearts when we're under crossfire.

Three Principles for Handling Relationship Pressures

1. Prioritize

When you find yourself in the crossfire, make some quick assessments to prioritize what you need to do. Try to pull off some sense of order in dealing with the crossfire.

First, turn to priority number one: your wife. You need her in the midst of these stressful times. You need her to help you sort through these hard times. You don't have to do it all alone.

Besides, you *can't* do it all alone. You can't do at once all the things that are facing you. (You may be good, but you aren't *that* good. Your wife, of course, can do seven or eight things simultaneously, but don't even try to keep up with her.)

Let's do some Monday-morning quarterbacking on a "hell week" in your life.

Think of one of your own crossfire times, when everything was happening at once and the pressure was coming from several directions. How did you prioritize your responses? What did you do first?

If you ask men like Officer Paul Bennett, the first thing you do under crossfire is to make sure your partner is covered. For us husbands, that means our wives.

But think about what happens in many marriages. In stressful times, the very person that God brought into a man's life to be his helper and partner often becomes perceived as his enemy. His wife tends to get more of our heat and less of our heart. Yet she, more than anyone else, needs to be plugged into his heart during the crossfire. She is his greatest asset in stressful times. She knows him the best and can step into the fire with him.

So when the stress of relational pressures hit, look to your copilot in life, your wife, to see how she's doing. Your marriage is your priority relationship. Siblings, parents, friends, and colleagues at work are important, but check the marriage front first to make certain you're on the same songsheet as your wife. Stay in touch with your lady.

Treat her like the partner she is, and remember that these pressure situations are growing times in your marriage that will bring you closer together.

Start by asking your wife one question: "What do you need from me?" Often we men think our wives need our solutions to the problem. In a full-blown crisis, yes, perhaps they do. But not in most situations. What they really need is our understanding.

Remember what Peter said in 1 Peter 3:7?

> Husbands, in the same way be considerate [understanding] as you live with your wives, and treat them with respect as the weaker partner and as heirs with you of the gracious gift of life, so that nothing will hinder your prayers.

We can show our understanding and consideration by tuning into their needs. How can we know those needs? Our wives may think we can read their minds, but we can't. We can, however, step up and ask the question, "Honey, what do you need from me right now?"

You take her temperature. Maybe she needs you to just plain listen as she unloads. Perhaps she could use a hug followed by a prayer. She may be asking you to give her some time to sort things out in her own mind (meaning that she can't solve it right away in a logical manner like you may be inclined to do).

And she may be asking you to defend her. (On that subject, let me give you a worthy piece of counsel: Don't stick up for the people she is feeling pressured by. There's time to do an autopsy on the pressure, but that's when you're out of the crisis, not in the middle of it.)

Here are some examples of what to say to her:

- How are you handling the stress of caring for your parents? I know you're hurting. I want to help; tell me how I can.
- What do you need from me as we deal with this painful time with our son?
- I'm sure the betrayal from your friend is painful for you. What can I do to help you right now?
- There are problems at your workplace. I know they're eating you alive. Let me in so I can come alongside you. What do you need me to do?
- I know the stress with your sister is putting you under the pile. What do you need most from me right now? A hug? A prayer? Some space? A walk?

The key in all such situations is to tune in to what your partner needs from you at that moment. It isn't that fancy. But it works.

Second, after finding out what she needs, share with her what *you're* needing. Maybe what you need most is simply for your wife to understand you. Or you may need some room and some time to sort things through (but be careful not to go into the cave and shut her out).

Sometimes, for a little reality check, I need Barb to let me express my thoughts. Expressing my feelings may come later, but not until I'm ready. (Feelings are higher risk, aren't they?) Maybe you're like that too.

There's almost a rhythm to it, don't you think? We start by verbalizing our thoughts, and if we feel we're being heard, then we may dip into the emotional side of the issue. Most of us men tend to pull back from the emotional side. We go for the thoughts and for the logic. We seem safer there. But our wives need us to dip into that emotional side. It puts us on a level playing field with them.

After you sense that you and your wife are on the same wavelength, then it's time to take a united front into the crossfire. You and your wife are a team—that's how God designed marriage. And a team doesn't work without both of you communicating constantly through the crossfire.

How you deal with your wife in this time of pressure will set the pace for how you deal with everyone and everything else. So I'll say it again: Priority numero uno is your lady. Make sure your wife's needs are being met first, for this relationship will impact everything else that happens.

Take one step at a time (keeping in step with your wife). Then get ready for more attacks, because the onslaught hasn't stopped.

To be honest, Barb and I have been in a crossfire the last several days. Things have heated up on all sides with the pressure of work, book-writing deadlines, kids' activities, and some relational conflicts to boot. Yesterday morning I got up after another too brief night of restless sleep, let my pooch out, grabbed a cup of coffee and my study Bible, and sat on the back porch drinking in a message from our Lord that was written just for me.

Listen to Paul in Romans 8:18-21.

> I consider that our present sufferings are not worth comparing with the glory that will be revealed in us. The creation waits in eager expectation for the sons of God to be revealed. For the creation was subjected to frustration, not by its own choice, but by the will of the one who subjected it, in hope that the creation itself will be liberated from its bondage to decay and brought into the glorious freedom of the children of God.

Sin has its consequences. In our fallen state we suffer. We feel the pain of illness, loss, and betrayal. We were born with a heart so deceived that when we take our eyes off God and let selfishness take over, our hearts become easy fodder for the enemy. That's why we need to guard our hearts: because our hearts are wicked at the core.

But here is the bright good news of this passage: One day, glory will be revealed to us. One day, in glory, there will be no more sin. Period. Instead, there will be glorious freedom.

That's the hope that we Christians have. All the illnesses, fears, anxieties, pressures, and crossfire will be gone. We will live in eternity with Jesus Christ. But until then, crossfire will keep coming.

2. Maintain peripheral vision

As you focus together on the biggest relationship crisis or dilemma in front of you, you can still at least note and monitor the needs in other relationships around you. Face firmly the big one, but don't completely ignore all the secondary issues that are raising their heads. That's where peripheral vision comes in.

Let's say your wife calls you in the middle of an important meeting at work with the news that her father has just been hospitalized and things look pretty serious. You kick into automatic pilot, assuring your wife on the phone that you're on your way, giving a thirty-second explanation to those in your office, and then heading out the door.

On the twenty-minute drive to meet your wife at the hospital, your mind starts flooding with "what ifs." *What if he doesn't pull through? What if my wife needs something from me I don't know how to give her? What if my kids get scared?*

As you pull into the parking lot, you see your five-year-old son looking out through the window of the emergency room waiting area. He looks big-eyed and pale—needing his dad.

Parking the car and running to the door you jump in with both feet. You embrace your wife, who is finally safe enough to let the tears flow. Your little boy is hanging onto your leg for dear life. You can deal with his needs, too, though not perhaps in as great a depth as your wife's. Your lady needs her knight's comfort and strength. Your son needs to know simply that Dad is there leading the charge. He needs your presence. And you need God's direction to stick to the task without tossing your own needs to the wind, but paying enough attention to your family's needs to give them the security-building knowledge that dad is on the job.

Jesus practiced this in a wonderful way in His earthly walk. On His way to heal Jairus's gravely ill daughter, the woman who had been bleeding for twelve years touched His cloak. Desperate for healing, she reached out to the One she believed would restore her to health. Jesus broke stride enough to turn to her and deal with her need before moving on with the distraught father.

Can you imagine Jairus's thoughts when Jesus stopped to heal the woman? Here Jairus was, leading the King of kings through the crowd, knowing in his heart that only Jesus could save his little girl. Then suddenly they came to a halt so Jesus could tend to a bleeding woman. Perhaps Jairus was saying inwardly, "Not now, Jesus. I'm afraid there won't be time. My little girl is dying. Please come now! Please hurry!"

Then, as Jesus miraculously healed the woman, Jairus's worst fears were realized:

> While Jesus was still speaking, some men came from the house of Jairus, the synagogue ruler. "Your daughter is dead," they said. "Why bother the teacher any more?"
>
> Ignoring what they said, Jesus told the synagogue ruler, "Don't be afraid; just believe." (Mark 5:35-36)

Can you sense the power those words must have had in Jairus's heart: "Don't be afraid; just believe." My friend, those are words recorded for the ages, for you and me.

Jairus believed, and his daughter was healed.

Jesus kept His focus on ministering to Jairus and his daughter. But that did not keep Him from ministering also to the bleeding woman. He understood the importance of maintaining peripheral vision. Even on the way to His death on Golgotha, carrying His own cross, He stopped to minister to some weeping women along His path. He's the Master, isn't He?

So when you're caught in the crossfire, you don't have to ignore other people, even if you don't have time to deal with their needs in depth.

Often it's enough for others simply to know that you've seen them, that you've acknowledged their need, that they aren't being ignored.

Assure them also that you will follow through:

"Listen, Jason, I know you need to talk about this, and I want to hear about it, too. But I've got to talk to your mom right now, and I promise I'll be down with you in about ten minutes, okay?"

Or, "Honey, I can't really deal with that on the phone right now. I have to meet with someone here in just a moment. Let's go out for dessert tonight and talk it through. Tom and Alyce can babysit for us. They owe us one. Okay?"

These statements aren't intended to blow off those who are needing you. To the contrary, they're intended to assure them of your interest in them and commitment to them—key ingredients in relationships.

The only variable you're trying to control is the *timing* of your discussion. But you still are committed to communicating, knowing that communication is absolutely necessary in relationships. When we stop communicating, we run the risk of significant misunderstandings.

You *must* follow through with these "appointments." Without follow-through you send the message that you can't be trusted, which always damages a relationship.

3. First aid first, non-emergency care later

If someone's hemorrhaging, you have to stop the bleeding. You deal with that and look after the bruises and sprains later.

There's a military principle of dividing battle casualties into three groups: the dead and dying, the seriously wounded, and the not seriously wounded. Medics know they can't help those who are dying, and the superficially wounded can hang in there. It's the seriously wounded who need immediate attention.

Who is hemorrhaging in your world today? Does someone in your life need the first aid that only you can deliver? Your wife? One of your children?

Jesus Christ Is Our Model

Look again at Jesus leading Jairus through the crowds, hastening to the man's home to heal his daughter. Jesus stopped to meet the immediate need of the bleeding woman. Why? Because she reached out to Him, and He showed his deep love and care for her.

There are people in your life reaching out right now for your attention. If you're anything like me, you may feel there are too many. Our wives, children, parents, friends, coworkers, neighbors—you name it, they have needs. When we're under this pressure and trying to balance all these relationships, sometimes we either blow up or pull away.

Here is my encouragement to you: *Step in* to the relationship. You don't have to do it perfectly, just willingly.

It starts with your wife. "Honey, I feel like I can't do it all. There is so much going on, and I feel overwhelmed by it. But I don't want to shut you out. I know you need to hear what I'm thinking, and especially what I'm feeling. Bear with me. This isn't always easy, but you need to know, and more importantly I know I need to tell you. I need you on my team. I want to start with you."

It isn't the easiest thing for men to face, but sometimes these hard times turn out to be some of the richest times of marriage and family life. The very stresses that divide us can also push us into closer relationship with our wives, allowing their tender sides to minister to ours. That's why it's so vital to be building our castles not on sand, but on the rock of healthy communication and deep respect and joint commitments.

Your family awaits. So does the crossfire. If you're under crossfire right now, the right response begins with walking into the room where your wife is and saying, "Honey, let's talk…."

If you aren't under crossfire now, the right thing to do is to build up your marriage relationship so your castle will stand strong when the storms rise up against it.

Relational crossfire doesn't have to take you out. You now have a plan—so go for it.

And remember: *Guard your heart.*

Application Suggestions:

1. When relational crossfire strikes next in your life, will you be ready to prioritize—to first make sure that your wife's needs are being met? If you are ready to do so, make a commitment to God to follow this guideline. On a sheet of paper, write down this commitment in your own words.

2. Below this commitment statement, write out your own paraphrase of 1 Peter 3:7. Do this by substituting you and your wife's first names for the words "husband" and "wife," then continuing to paraphrase the rest of the verse in this way.

3. What could you *say* to your wife the next time you are experiencing "relational crossfire"? As good practice, write down five possible ways that you could genuinely express support and encouragement to her.

4. Once again, think about the truth outlined in Philippians 4:6-7— *PRAYING thoroughly and with thanksgiving about everything (instead of worrying) leads to the PEACE of God, which will GUARD YOUR HEART and mind in Christ Jesus.* Write out a prayer to God that sincerely expresses your desire for His help in facing relational pressures, and for putting your wife's interests first.

To Think About & Discuss:

1. In Psalm 31:4-13, David describes an emotional crossfire that sent him into a season of deep distress. What helpful perspective did David gain in verses 14-15 and 21-22 that enabled him to endure...and even rejoice? What counsel does he give fellow believers who find themselves in a similar crossfire (verses 23-24)?

2. Now take a moment to read about some crossfire the apostle Paul experienced in 2 Corinthians 1:8-9 and 7:5-7. Speculate on the sorts of things he might have been wrestling with in verse 5 of chapter 7. In what ways can you identify with this description? What remedy did the God of comfort bring across the apostle's path? How can you find—and be— such a remedy?

3. For a rich, extended study, consider Elijah's crossfire and resulting depression. Read his complaint to the Lord from the dank depths of a dark cave in 1 Kings 19:9-10. What specific things did the Lord do for His discouraged servant in verses 11-18? In what way was our Lord's dealing with Elijah in the latter part of verse 16 similar to His dealing with Paul in the 2 Corinthians passage cited above?

CHAPTER EIGHT

FRONTAL ATTACK #4:
SEXUAL TEMPTATION

.

A number of years ago, as a young professional, I was visiting with a man we'll call Roger. He was an executive of a large corporation, and as a man just getting started in my own career, I have to admit I was taken with this guy.

Roger had it all. He'd received national recognition for his work, had a beautiful little family, and a sterling reputation in the community. Since I was visiting that part of the country, Roger generously agreed to meet with me and give me a little career counseling. I was extremely nervous as the meeting began, but Roger's gracious, brotherly welcome soon put me at ease.

As we sat and talked, I admired the posh decor of his office: solid oak furniture, plush carpeting, leather upholstery. Yet the most vivid memory I have of our visit wasn't Roger's counsel, the decor, or his kindness to a young man trying to launch a profession.

Over the two-hour meeting, I was transfixed by a large, elegantly framed print hanging over his desk. A feeling of warmth and admiration for this man welled up within me as I looked at that painting. To me, it indicated a brother willing to stand tall for what he believed.

You may have seen the print I'm speaking of. It portrays an executive in his fifties, sitting in his office, and speaking intently with a visitor. The chair across the desk, however, isn't occupied by a young professional seeking wisdom or a client seeking counsel. It's occupied by Jesus Christ.

To me, the "sermon" was as eloquent as it was silent. We need to live as if Jesus Christ was visibly present in our study, our office, or our home. I stood up after the meeting and went over to look more closely at the picture. I remember being struck by the sincere look on the executive's face, and by the compassionate look of Jesus. I was so impressed that a man like Roger—a man in his position, with his influence—would so unashamedly display such a painting, right there in his office for all eyes to see.

Maybe someday, I thought, *I could be that secure in my faith.*

More about Roger later.

Scott's Story

Unlike Roger, Scott did not display his faith overtly. Scott came to me for counsel, and as he walked through the door, I knew he was in some kind of deep trouble. He was ashen. Shaken. I took a deep breath, shot up a quick prayer, and asked him to sit down.

"I didn't think it could ever happen. We were just friends," Scott said. "She was going through a hard time when I met her through work, and honest to God, Gary, *we were just friends.*"

I couldn't help sighing. I already knew where this conversation was going.

"Nothing happened," he went on, "at least…for a long time. We'd—you know—just have lunch, to talk about how things were going with her and her husband, Rick. Then I found myself opening up about Susan and some of the hassles I was having at home. One day at lunch, I looked up at her and there was something different. The way she was looking at me—she was so intent. I couldn't figure it out at first, but then it hit me. She really cared. She was really interested in what I was saying. I think that's where I took the wrong turn. The more we talked, the more I felt like—like some kind of high school kid discovering a girl for the first time. I haven't felt like that in years. Maybe Susan and I used to have that kind of chemistry, but—well, I guess over the years of paying bills, raising kids, and all the pressures…we've lost it.

"We began to laugh, and an hour lunch turned into a three-hour time together that—well, just happened. I didn't plan it. It got out of hand so fast. I can't believe it. From lunch to private meetings. From looks to touches. By the time we met for the first time in the hotel it was like the most natural next step. It seemed like the thing to do. My body was raging and I couldn't think of anything else. It wasn't planned, Gary. It really wasn't. It just happened. Like a freight train out of control."

"Does Susan know about this, Scott?" I asked.

"Oh yeah, Susan knows all right." He sighed deeply and ran a hand across his face. "She wants to—take the kids and leave. I can't believe what's happening! It's a nightmare. I don't know what to tell her. My dad always taught me to stay faithful. My life is over. At least the life I've always known. If only I could go back! If only I hadn't let this thing get started! I didn't mean to hurt anyone."

Two men. Roger, with a satisfying profession, family, stature in his field. The works. A guy who wasn't afraid to display a painting of Jesus Christ right over his desk for all to see. Then Scott, a younger man who also had so much, including right teaching by a loving dad, but threw away a lifetime of commitment for a few minutes of hormonal stimulation. My heart went out to him. He was scared, panicky, and facing terrible hurdles to restore his marriage.

Scott Isn't Alone

I can't tell you the number of "Scotts" who have sat in my office. It makes me weary to think about it. When we allow sexual temptation to scale our castle walls, we set ourselves up for the fall of a lifetime.

Although the men in my survey rated sexual temptation as the fourth major threat to the safety of their castle (which frankly surprised me), research indicates that men are falling into adultery in unprecedented numbers. Non-Christians and Christians alike. One reputable source indicated that forty to fifty percent of all married men have extramarital affairs. For men under age forty, the figure rises to seventy percent.

Look around you. For every ten guys you see in the office, in your shop, on your softball team, or in your Sunday school class, four to five of them have fallen. About half of all men are either living with what they think are private lies, or have actually left their marriage, or are trying to rebuild trust destroyed by adultery.

Am I employing scare tactics here? Maybe. But it's no exaggeration to say that we men are vulnerable. We're wired with sex on our minds much of the day. In the book *His Needs, Her Needs,* Willard Harley says that the number one need for men is sex. Well, if that's our number one need, then where do you think Satan would hit guys to get us to stumble? Is it any surprise men are being hammered in this area? Satan may work very hard at what he does, but I don't think he's into wasting effort. Why should he come up with unique and innovative plans for tripping up men, when the techniques he's used for thousands of years still work? Sexual temptation is still his weapon of choice...and why not? It still works.

As men we tend to "sexualize" things. Smells, touch, sight—you name it—it tends to go through a sexual filter. It's been said that the typical guy thinks about sex several times each hour. In his new book *The Sexual Man,* Archibald Hart says that 16% of the men he studied reported thinking about sex hourly, while more than 61% answered "daily." That adds up to nearly four out of every five men. Whether it is several times per hour or per day, that's a lot of masculine thought power being given to sex. With such a preoccupation with sex, how do men get any work done?

It's no coincidence that many men fall in this area. But falling into sexual sin is rarely a fluke. Healthy relationships and healthy choices don't just "go bad" all at once. Relationships don't collapse, they *erode.*

In the same way, extramarital affairs rarely happen overnight. Adulterous relationships tend to develop over time when we become emotionally vulnerable and are growing distant from our wives. Then, at precisely the wrong time —when our vigilance is weak and our defenses are down—the enemy presents us with...an opportunity.

Adultery doesn't just happen. Men don't suddenly walk away from a marriage commitment like an ox to the slaughter. My friend Scott tried to tell me he'd been hit by a runaway freight train. But the truth is, it took a lot of time for that train to build up momentum, and he'd done nothing to slow it down. The time to stop a train, of course, is when it starts chugging down the wrong tracks.

Adultery has to begin somewhere, doesn't it? And it doesn't begin in the perfumed darkness of a hotel room. It doesn't begin over cocktails at Hernando's Hideaway in an obscure part of town. It doesn't begin with little flirtations in the office hallway.

It begins in the heart.

It begins with a single thought in an unguarded moment.

The momentum builds from there.

But how do we keep from caving into the temptation in the first place? How do we build healthy protections into our lifestyle? Why are men falling left and right—Christian leaders, friends, family members? Why does adultery claim so many men? Listen to the words of Solomon in Proverbs 5, the chapter that follows our "guard your heart" passage in Proverbs 4.

What a Real Expert Says

> My son, pay attention to my wisdom,
>   listen well to my words of insight,
> that you may maintain discretion
>   and your lips may preserve knowledge.
> For the lips of an adulteress drip honey,
>   and her speech is smoother than oil. (5:1-3)

Once again, a father is instructing his son. He is warning his son of the danger of an adulterous woman. A dad is telling his boy to make good choices so that his witness remains true:

- Walk into life with both eyes open.
- Stick to the course, son.
- Remain faithful so that your character stays intact.
- Be sold out to the wife of your youth.
- Finish the race.

Who is this adulteress who beckons the man? Her lips "drip honey" (the sweetest substance in ancient Israel) and her speech is "smoother than oil" (the smoothest substance).

Solomon is writing about a prostitute.

Many of you sit back and say, "Hey, Gary, I would never go with a prostitute." That's most likely the case. But she doesn't have to be a prostitute; most men don't fall to prostitutes. They fall to the woman who steps into their life "out of nowhere." Whether she's a prostitute or the woman next door, she's enticing. She knows what to say. She knows all the moves. She knows how to hook a man.

But Solomon continues.

> In the end she is bitter as gall,
> sharp as a double-edged sword.
> Her feet go down to death;
> her steps lead straight to the grave.
> She gives no thought to the way of life;
> her paths are crooked, but she knows it not. (5:4-6)

Pretty fleeting delight, isn't it? From lips that "drip honey" and smooth speech to becoming "bitter as gall" and "sharp as a double-edged sword." There are consequences to sexual sin. We not only run the risk of disease and of killing our marriages, but we also open ourselves up to another person and become one with her in body, emotion, soul, and mind. We share a part of us that is to be guarded and given to one woman only: our wife. When you go to bed with another woman, you're not only acting selfishly and wounding your own marriage; but you're also killing hers—or the future marriage God may be preparing her for. The damage is incalculable.

Solomon goes on to write:

> Now then, my son, listen to me:
> do not turn aside from what I say.
> Keep to a path far from her,
> do not go near the door of her house,
> lest you give your best strength to others
> and your years to one who is cruel,
> lest strangers feast on your wealth
> and your toil enrich another man's house. (5:9-10)

By failing to walk or run from temptation, we lose. We lose strength, self-respect, health, security, safety. We embrace a life of regret.

And that's why we need guardrails.

Guardrails

Have you ever traveled on a mountain road? Maybe in the Rockies, or the Smokies, or the Cascades? When I get on those roads, I'm always thankful that the higher up you go, the more guardrails there are.

Guardrails are there for a purpose. Not to box you in and stymie you or keep you from admiring the scenery, but to protect you from plunging over the edge. When I drive those mountain roads with yawning cliffs scant inches away from the edge of the pavement, I tend to slow down. I don't want to drink a Pepsi with one hand, fiddle with the radio with the other, and steer with my knees. I like both hands on the wheel and both eyes glued to that little white line in the middle of the road. I may not be the smartest guy in the world, but I'm not a fool, either. I don't want to play Mario Andretti, racing around curves and cliffs at 7,000 feet above sea level.

How do I drive in those mountain passes? I drive with great caution, and I thank God for the guardrails.

The same is true when we risk plunging over the cliff edge of adultery. When we find ourselves in an area of danger, when we sense that "still small voice" of God's Spirit warning us, we must begin to move with great—even exaggerated—caution. We need to keep both eyes straight ahead of us. And we need to let God's guardrails protect us.

Let me suggest four guardrails for your consideration.

Guardrail #1: A strong relationship with the Father

Go back to Solomon's words in the opening verses of Proverbs 5:

> My son, pay attention to my wisdom,
>   listen well to my words of insight,
> that you may maintain discretion
>   and your lips may preserve knowledge. (5:1-2)

Solomon's warning is rich with instruction. Listen to the words he emphasizes: "wisdom," "insight," "discretion." Who is the author of all this fatherly instruction? The greatest Father of all.

My friend, our relationship with the Father is our strongest guardrail. He has the best counsel. He knows exactly how men—and women—are put together. He cares about the things we men think about. He is vitally interested and concerned about where we put our focus. How we deal with our sexuality is of utmost importance to Him. Listen to these words from Paul:

> Finally, brothers, whatever is true, whatever is noble, whatever is right, whatever is pure, whatever is lovely, whatever is admirable— if anything is excellent or praiseworthy—think about such things. (Philippians 4:8)

Do you know what verse precedes this challenge? Listen to verse seven:

> And the peace of God, which transcends all understanding, will *guard your hearts and your minds in Christ Jesus.*

Inviting God to examine our thoughts will always push us toward purity. It means that we allow both the Word of God and our frequent conversations with Him to weave a web of discipline and protection around our most private thoughts. As Paul expressed it to the Corinthians, "Take each thought captive for Christ" (2 Corinthians 10:5).

If you are allowing sinful thoughts and images to linger on the screen of your mind, then know that they will find a final resting place in your heart. If you are reading, watching, and thinking about sexual images that are dishonoring to God, then take those thoughts captive and march them at sword point before the King for trial and execution.

If the thoughts have actually moved you from fantasies to the threshold of an illicit relationship, you need the next guardrail.

Guardrail #2: An extreme caution with other women

Back to Proverbs 5, verses 3-11. This is where Solomon describes the adulteress whose lips "drip with honey." He has one clear message: *Keep a path far from her.*

Simple counsel, isn't it? But there really isn't a better, truer word than that.

As Scott described earlier in this chapter, adultery doesn't start off with sexual behaviors. It often starts far more innocuously through a look, a word, a touch. It then accelerates into an emotional relationship which builds momentum toward disaster and despair.

Let me ask you a direct question: *Where are you involving yourself with another woman who could set you up to fall?* Be brutally honest with yourself. Don't rationalize with me on this one, friend. If you are exposed to a woman in your life—whether at work, church, or anywhere else—who prompts your mind to impure thoughts, then take a hike, Mike. Do *everything possible* to stay clear from her. Even at the risk of offending her. Even at the risk of embarrassing yourself. These are mild risks compared to the risk of adultery and a shattered marriage. If you are in a meeting with her and find that you are focusing on her in an impure way, then quickly do two things.

First (if circumstances keep you from physically leaving the room), choose to shift the focus away from her by thinking of your own wife. Pray for your kids and wife. Pray for this woman's family, too. Pray for her relationship with God. Illicit sexual thoughts don't easily coexist with sincere prayer.

Second, take the step of avoiding future meetings with her. Some of you may be sitting back saying, "Hey Rosberg, that is a little extreme." So is the potential loss of your family and honor. Your life story may depend upon your move here, friend. Is it worth it?

Some men tell me they find themselves lingering after public meetings with women they're attracted to. If that's the case, invite your wife to those meetings. If she can't go, then invite a male friend and avoid any one-on-one time with the woman. If you work with such a woman, set strict boundaries for yourself, and do whatever possible to minimize any private time with her. An ounce of prevention is worth a pound, or better yet, a *ton* of cure.

How about touch? We all touched a lot in my family. Touch is important to me. I like to shake my buddies' hands and slap their backs. I touch my wife and kids all the time. Our families need our touch. But the confusion sets in when men touch women who are not their wives. My wife tells me that when a man touches a woman, it means something different to her than it does to him. Casual as it might seem to you, it's an intimate gesture to her.

Solution? Easy. *You touch your wife and I'll touch mine.* Does that mean I never touch another woman in greeting? No…but I am very, very cautious. I don't need the headaches of misunderstanding. Do you? Here's how I measure what's appropriate in touching a woman: If my wife, daughters, and mother could all be in the room observing and would each give me the "thumbs up sign" without a check in their own spirits on my behavior, then it's okay.

We can rationalize our behaviors, thoughts, and feelings regarding other women until the cows come home. (That's an Iowa expression. One per book is my limit.) But God knows your heart. Allow him to examine all of your ways, friend. Flee from any woman in your path who could lead you and your precious family to destruction. Your life story hangs in the balance.

Guardrail #3: A wide-open relationship with our brothers

Our friends can also serve as a strong guardrail of sexual purity in our lives. But we have to tell them we're struggling if they can ever be able to help us! And that means we need men in our lives who love us enough to challenge us in the private areas of our thoughts. It means we need men to whom we can confess our hearts.

> Therefore confess your sins to each other and pray for each other
> so that you may be healed. The prayer of a righteous man is
> powerful and effective. (James 5:16)

Having good, solid male relationships helps protect our castle on three fronts when it comes time to deal with the issue of sexual purity.

First, these men can be there to encourage us up front to remain pure. We need to be asking hard questions of each other and holding each other strictly accountable in this critical area.

Second, they can be there to edify us when we are struggling with sin in our lives. Good friends can keep their antenna up to see if we are drifting into dangerous territory with other women. They can also ask us those questions that go straight for the heart:

- Is that woman you spoke of filling your thoughts during the day? How often do you think about her?
- Have you entertained any impure thoughts about other women since we last talked?
- What situations are leading you into times of impure thoughts? TV? Nights at home alone? Trips to the convenience store to hang out at the magazine rack?

Have you begun stepping into areas that could lead to your downfall? If so, confess it to your brother. Let him throw you a lifeline.

Third, brothers can help restore our lives if we have not remained pure and have blown right through the guardrails. Our culture lies to us. IT says men don't need each other that much, and that men aren't capable of sustaining meaningful friendships anyway. Neither is true. We *do* need each other and we *can* encourage and strengthen each other in deeply significant ways. *Real men need other men.*

I'm reminded of a little incident when I was in Albuquerque, not long ago, teaching a marriage conference. I was doing this one solo, leaving Barb behind to be a mom to the girls.

I was in my room reviewing my notes when I received a call from Mark Schatzman, who was responsible for marketing the conference. We hadn't met before, but he gave me a call and asked if I was hungry. I'm always hungry, so he invited me down to his room for some Chinese food.

In his room I couldn't help but notice a bath towel draped over his TV set. *Now that's an interesting place to hang your towel,* I thought. *Well, maybe he's not the neatest guy in the world and that's where it landed. Or maybe when the TV heats up, it dries out the towel.*

After some mediocre Chinese food and great conversation, I returned to my room to crash for the night. The next morning as I passed the front desk, a woman behind the counter asked if I could give Mr. Schatzman a message.

When I delivered the message to Mark, he smiled.

The message was: "Where is your towel?"

Mark read the question on my face and took a moment to fill in the blanks.

He and some friends had made a commitment to put towels over hotel TV sets to protect themselves from temptation on the road. Realizing that temptation goes up when the presence of others goes down, this was a way for them to hold each other accountable.

No big deal, maybe. Just a little band of soldiers standing guard for each other. Just a few guys who've decided to go the extra mile to stay pure…and to walk that mile together.

Then again, what is a victorious life but a series of little victorious skirmishes? These men are committed to each other for the long haul.

Guardrail #4: A fulfilling relationship with our wife

Solomon phrased it this way (in Proverbs 5:15-19):

> Drink water from your own cistern,
>   running water from your own well…
> May your fountain be blessed,
>   and may you rejoice in the wife of your youth.
> A loving doe, a graceful deer—
>   may her breasts satisfy you always,
>   may you be ever captivated with her love.

In other words, if you're sexually thirsty, head for your own well. The well God has provided for you. Quench your thirst at your own fountain, instead of roaming around looking for another. When we are satisfied from *drinking in* life with our own wife, then we'll never need to search outside that relationship for satisfaction.

I call this experiencing *intimacy*. The word *intimate* comes from the Latin word, *intimus,* which means *"innermost."* In *The Pursuit of Intimacy,* authors David Fergueson and Chris Thurman define intimacy as "that gnawing of the soul for emotional and spiritual connectedness with our Creator and other human beings." C. M. Rubenstein and P. Shaver in their book *In Search of Intimacy,* write this:

> Psychologists have evolved their own list of defining features for
> intimacy: openness, honesty, mutual self disclosure, caring,
> warmth, protecting, helping, being devoted to each other,
> mutually attentive, mutually committed, surrendering control,

dropping defenses, becoming emotionally attached, and feeling distressed when separation occurs.

These terms may sound to you like something from outer space, but if you dare to ask your wife if they have meaning to her, she'll happily go to the moon with you. When we pursue intimacy with our wives we're speaking their language. Our wives thirst for our caring and warmth. It's what women dream of with their man… an emotional, spiritual, and sexual oneness that meets the craving in their soul to be connected, protected, cared for, and cherished. And when we as men step up to the plate and begin to look at the potential for marriages that involve intimacy, marriages change. Not overnight, but little by little the guardrails go up and we don't even begin to look outside of them for anything or anyone to meet those needs.

You see, you don't need other women or images of other women to soothe your soul. The woman you met at the end of the wedding aisle would walk across America to receive you if you took a shot at building intimacy in your marriage. In two words: *It works.* In two more words: *Try it.*

I've learned a lot from listening to men all around the country. And one thing that really rings true is that when men turn back to their wives and begin to drink from their *own cisterns,* relationships get solid. Castle walls become protective again. The fun in the family returns as moms, dads, and kids feel safer to laugh, to talk, even to goof up. People relax in the safety of their castles. Life becomes rich again, rather than burdensome. Home becomes a haven rather than a hassle.

And you and I as men hold the key to building those relationships.

The Long-Range Impact of a Short-Range Decision

What's the impact of giving in to the lust of the flesh? Let's go back to the wisdom of the Bible.

Solomon wrote,

> At the end of your life you will groan,
>   when your flesh and body are spent.
> You will say, "How I hated discipline!

> How my heart spurned correction!
> I would not obey my teachers
> or listen to my instructors.
> I have come to the brink of utter ruin
> in the midst of the whole assembly." (Proverbs 5:11-14)

I can't imagine the pain that a father who committed sexual sin—as David did with Bathsheba—must have felt as he was trying to help his son avert the pain of his own behavior. David knew what it felt like. Sadly, Solomon also learned about the incredible devastation of sexual activity without boundaries.

The long-range consequences include guilt, regret, and loss of intimacy, to name a few. At the end of life, it will be too late to seek guardrails. We need them *now*. Now, while life still stretches out ahead of us. Now, while there's still time to make a difference in our family, hold out a light to our culture, and bring eternal glory to Christ.

That's why we men must guard our hearts. We must learn from the pitfalls of those who have stumbled on the path ahead of us.

The Rest of Roger's Story

Remember Roger, the man with the picture of Jesus in his office?

Several years after our visit, a friend told me that Roger chose an adulterous relationship with a customer, a woman who began to meet with him in his office...right under that picture of Jesus Christ.

The office meetings led to hotel encounters, and—ultimately—the death of two families. Roger and his female friend both rejected the guardrails of their spouses, churches, and kids, and moved in with each other.

The result? Roger lost his business. He lost his trappings of success. He lost his witness. And I can't help but wonder—what happened to the painting that so captivated me?

Hey, paintings of Christ are fine. A Bible plaque on your wall is great. Fish lapel pins are cool. Christian bumper stickers have their place. Christian books on the bookshelf are certainly worthwhile. But listen...the external trappings of Christianity won't cut it when you step into a war zone. The undertow of sexual sin is *way* too strong. If you're weak, it will yank you right off your feet and pull you out to sea—way over your head.

All those things I mentioned are good and worthy items. But they are without power to help you. They're just externals. We dare not use them as talismans or charms. And they will never serve as guardrails. We need truth, power, and love. The truth of God's strong Word. The power and wisdom of God's Holy Spirit. And the love of God, our families, and brothers who walk with us, shoulder to shoulder.

A Warning Sign

This chapter could be a warning sign for you, or perhaps it's a mirror. You may be real uncomfortable right now. If you've given in to the temptation of sexual sin, I implore you to do something about it. Start with stopping. *Now.* God can restore you to Himself. God can walk you through each step of this thing. He promises to be faithful.

If you haven't fallen, but are looking over the edge of the cliff, then back away. *Now.* Run, friend. Go home. Go home to your wife and kids. Seek out a brother or pastor or professional counselor to help you work through this swamp…no matter how deep in the mud you may be.

There is hope.

There is forgiveness.

There is enough power to be all He's called us to be.

Let's guard our hearts.

Application Suggestions:

1. Look back at the four "guardrails" mentioned in this chapter. On a sheet of paper, write down all four of them. Under each one, write a one-sentence or one-paragraph plan of what you will decide to do *in the next ten days* to strengthen your protection in this area. Make your plan simple and achievable—but make sure it's truly significant and helpful as well.

2. Is there anything you need to *stop* in a relationship with another woman? Commit yourself before God to stop *now.*

3. Again, think about the pattern in Philippians 4:6-7—*PRAYING thoroughly and with thanksgiving about everything… which leads to the PEACE of God… which will GUARD YOUR HEART and mind in Christ Jesus.* Write out a prayer to God that sincerely expresses your desire for His help in resisting sexual temptation.

To Think About & Discuss:

1. Open your Bible to Genesis 39 and review a young man's experience with a woman determined to seduce him. In what specific ways did Joseph resist her advances? What lessons can we learn from Joseph's actions?

2. Read Proverbs 7:6-23. How might the "guardrails" described in this chapter have kept this foolish young man from destroying his life in adultery?

3. The author quotes James 5:16 to emphasize the strong guardrail of a relationship with caring, concerned brothers. Though James was speaking to the issue of physical healing in the verse, how might it also apply to spiritual and emotional healing as we struggle with this issue of sexual purity?

4. In what ways could Proverbs 5:15-19 speak to a man toying with pornography, sexually explicit movies, or impure thought patterns?

....

CHAPTER NINE

Sneak Attack #1:
The Search
for Significance

.

S uccess.

Its definitions are as varied as those who pursue it.

Aristotle Onassis, tycoon: "It's not a question of money. After you reach a certain point, money becomes unimportant. What matters is success. The sensible thing would be for me to stop now. But I can't. I have to keep aiming higher and higher—just for the thrill."

Barbara Streisand, recording artist: "Success for me is having ten honeydew melons and eating only the top half of each one."

Ted Turner, media mogul: "Well, I think it's kind of an empty bag, to tell you the truth, but you have to really get there to really know that. I've always said I was more an adventurer than I was a businessman. I mainly did CNN just to see if it would work. And the same with the superstation... Just out of personal curiosity to see if it could be done."

Helen Hayes, Broadway star: "My mother drew a distinction between achievement and success. She said that achievement is the knowledge that you have studied and worked hard and done the best that is in you. Success is being praised by others, and that's nice, too, but not as important or satisfying. Always aim for achievement, and forget about success."

Some people phrase it this way: "I want to leave the world a better place after I leave." Others say, "I want to make my mark." And still others, "I want to be remembered for something."

Many of us have moved up corporate ladders faster, made money earlier, and peaked out quicker than our fathers before us. But there is a price to this sometimes frantic pursuit of an elusive goal. By the time many folks come to my office for marriage and family counseling, they've already been levied with the bill…and they wonder if they can pay.

As a counselor I've sat and talked with countless people from all walks of life. I've met with business executives, professionals from every field imaginable, and up and coming young entrepreneurs. I've listened to men and women who earn high incomes, travel the world, and sport eye-popping credentials. Yet in their most vulnerable moments, many of these movers and shakers frankly admit they've lost what really counts: peace of mind and heart.

Many who've spent years pursuing success now feel themselves pursued— by a nightmare. What seemed like a climb up a ladder becomes a jump into a hole of despair. Alcohol and drugs may become the way out, and all sense of purpose is lost. These are people who expected to succeed—and did—only to find their lives filled with endless activity, futility, and emotional turmoil.

At the root of this dilemma are two competing views: our culture's view of success, and God's view of significance.

The Endless Pursuit

As men, much of the success we experience is tied to our work, our profession. The elements of work and success seem interwoven. Why do we work? Yes, to pay the bills and keep food on the table. But there are other reasons. The truth is, work feeds our craving for recognition and success.

These days we want jobs that will allow us to *express ourselves*…that will help fill our ego and identity needs. We also want work that is *challenging and fulfilling*. What else do we want? To be *in control*.

We all have an ego, a perspective of ourselves. Some egos are as big as a barn. Others are under the pile. But make no mistake, we all have one. Our ego or identity is who we are and how we see ourselves. A fulfilling job is one way of expressing those ego and identity needs. Our work helps define us. But it is when work becomes our *primary purpose* that we begin to get confused about this issue.

Men are often so sold on the idea that "I am what I do" that they lose all sense of balance. We claw our way up the promotion list, develop our careers, and sacrifice our families, looking for someone to finally tell us we're okay, that we've done enough, that we've earned enough, that we're now successful. But we know deep in our souls that enough is never enough. That when we finish this project, another one waits right behind it. There's always a smarter, faster, better-trained someone waiting just around the corner.

I remember traveling to Seattle once with my first boss after college, Bernie Vogelgesang. We were sitting at an airport gate waiting for a flight. Bernie was in his late forties at the time, and highly regarded in the field of adult corrections. I was about twenty-two. Neither of us dreamed that in a couple of years he would be dead of cancer, a cancer already eating away at his body.

"You know Gary," he said, "when I was your age they used to call me a bright young man. Then I hit my thirties, and they called me a bright man. Now that I'm in my forties, do you know what they call me? Just one of the boys."

We laughed. But now that I'm in my forties, I know what he means.

Perspectives change as we age. Success in my twenties seemed to be defined as upward mobility within a given company or profession. But now, in my forties, the shine has disappeared from the apple. Now I'm looking for something deeper and more enduring than a surfacey kind of success.

Meeting our ego needs through work and worldly standards of success is a risky venture. It's a lot like gambling. You may get on a lucky roll and stack up your winnings for a while, but ultimately you're going to lose. It's only a matter of time. You'll be sitting at the table in your boxer shorts without a chip to your name. When the corporation downsizes, when the sales force is cut, when your company moves to cut its overhead…your job will be affected and your ego is going to get hammered.

Success is not the yardstick with which to measure your self-worth and ego needs. It's too fleeting and unpredictable.

How About "Performance"?

We grew up doing piano recitals, trying to get hits in Little League, and striving for good grades. Often the need to seek the approval of others—such as our parents—established patterns of a performance-based lifestyle. And as we grow, we really don't shift much from those ingrained patterns. We keep on trying to achieve, achieve, achieve.

We so often define our worth based upon our performance. If we score high in those areas we're especially concerned about, then we're worthy. But as someone has well said: "The man or woman who lives only for the love and attention of others is never satisfied—as least, not for long." Why doesn't the satisfaction last? Because it's trying to fill a void within us by *outside* sources, sources that will never endure.

What happens when we can't perform well enough for the perfectionist in our life who is evaluating us? It may be a boss with excruciating expectations, a spouse who's never pleased, or a dad who still won't give you the approval you strive for.

And for some men, the worst taskmaster is someone else.

It's *you*. Your own unrealistic expectations are eating you alive.

There's nothing wrong with setting goals and performing with excellence. What I'm addressing here is that when we become performance-driven, we end up basing our self-worth on our ability to accomplish a goal. But then, when that goal isn't met for one reason or another, we see ourselves as a failure, as unworthy, as unacceptable.

Friend, you don't need other people's perfectionism. You also don't need your own. A perfectionist or performance-based person will eat you alive. If *you're* the perfectionist, then you'll eat *yourself* alive.

Realize that you need to draw a line and say, "Enough! I'm UNWILLING to burn myself alive trying to measure up to some arbitrary expectation. I'm UNWILLING to allow your expectation of me to define who I am. I'm UNWILLING to have my success or lack of success determine my worth and significance. I'm going to seek that elsewhere. Where it counts. In my relationship with my Lord, who gave me worth."

A Sadder But Wiser Man Speaks Again

Our friend King Solomon tried to fill his ego needs through his compulsive lifestyle. Remember, he had it all. He was a king, an author, a builder, a diplomat, a trader, a patron of the arts, and a collector. Yet in spite of all the wisdom with which he was blessed, he turned away from the Lord in his frenetic search for happiness and fulfillment. He lived life with his foot to the floorboard and every fantasy at his fingertips, yet he remains one of the most graphic examples in Scripture of a man steeped in regret. As we have already mentioned, Solomon's last writings reflect a man in the grip of profound pain and remorse.

> So I hated life, because the work that is done under the sun was grievous to me. All of it is meaningless, a chasing after the wind. I hated all the things I had toiled for under the sun. (Ecclesiastes 2:17)

His lack of contentment in the things of this world are freely displayed in his writing. Solomon concludes that the more we emphasize our human "successes," the more futile our lives will become. On the other hand, the more we emphasize our relationship with God, the more we will be fulfilled and content.

The final verses in Ecclesiastes 12 read:

> Now all has been heard: Here is the conclusion of the matter. Fear God and keep his commandments, for this is the whole duty of man. For God will bring every deed into judgment, including every hidden thing, whether it is good or evil. (2:13-14)

Do you hear Solomon? Do you hear this man who'd make Donald Trump look like a kid at a Kool-Aid stand? God is the only cure for the gnawing of the soul! No amount of material success, sensual pleasure, or earthly achievement can fill the bill.

Men, we all have a need. A need to be significant. A need to be loved, to love, and to be accepted not for what we do, but for who we are. Success is fleeting. Significance—our standing with our Creator—is forever. Significance comes in a relationship, a relationship with the God-man, Jesus Christ. It's who *He* is that allows us to take an inside look and say, "I have meaning. I have worth. I am of value."

Your heart is really the issue. If it's open and willing, God can touch your life and direct you. If it is hardened and closed, then step into the line for the roller coaster. Our culture's view of success will take you up, down, and around in circles, and deposit you no further than where you began.

Let's see how we can make the shift from a success-driven lifestyle to a life that aims for significance.

How to Redefine Success

As the pace of life screams out of control, real men are stepping back and saying, "Okay, give me an alternative." Rather than dropping out, wearing gold chains, and moving to the beach or hills to find themselves, they're saying, "Help me realize that I can still find some fulfillment in my work, but also pay attention to matters of the heart. How do I find a way to succeed in the marketplace and still keep my relationships and my own personal growth intact?"

Part of the answer is to redefine success. Success is not just a matter of money, power, and ego, but also issues of the heart—like compassion, kindness, bravery, generosity, love.

It's an issue of character, not performance.

It's an issue of being the person God designed you to be, not how much salary you can pull down in a year.

It's an issue of who you really are, not how many notches you can rack up on your resume or the shape of your car's hood ornament.

A recent *Time* magazine article called "The Simple Life" had this to say:

> After a ten-year bender of gaudy dreams and godless consumerism, Americans are starting to trade down. They want to reduce their attachments to status symbols, fast-track careers and great expectations of Having It All. Upscale is out; downscale is in.
>
> In place of materialism, many Americans are embracing simpler pleasures and homier values. They've been thinking hard about what really matters in their lives, and they've decided to make some changes. What matters is having time for family and friends, rest and recreation, good deeds and spirituality.

Not bad from *Time*, wouldn't you say?

A Value Shift to Significance

Values are what undergird our day-to-day thoughts, behaviors, and attitudes. They form our belief systems about our lives and are foundational to how we see the world. Our values once came predominantly from our training in the home and church. But in my generation, those values underwent an incredible shake-up in the turbulent sixties. From race riots to Woodstock, we challenged everything our parents stood for. Stability, perseverance, and moral absolutes were replaced with "letting it all hang out" and "doing whatever comes natural." The Who sang the song "My Generation" with the lyrics "Hope I die before I get old." Our whole value system was overturned, shaking not only our own lives, but our children's as well.

And now the bills have come due. Our culture is without a firm foundation. We're on shaky ground.

The answer is a change back to the values and truths that have stood the test of time: a biblical value system that works. A shift from success to significance.

Who makes us significant? I believe it is a Person. Not your boss, kids, parents, or even you. What makes you and I significant is the Person of Jesus Christ. He created us in order to glorify Himself. That's our job in life, to bring honor and glory to *Him*. He is the One who makes us significant. When we grab hold of this truth, then what others may think about us or our performance takes its proper place in our lives.

I like the way Paul put it to his friends in Galatia:

> Am I trying now to win the approval of men, or of God? Or am I trying to please men? If I were still trying to please men, I would not be a servant of Christ. (Galatians 1:10)

Yes, I care what others think about me. But it's not everything. It's not all-important. Sure, I'd like to have others like me and respect me, but not at the cost of my integrity. I heard a respected and nationally known pastor say one time, "My integrity doesn't have to be defended."

If I have to be all things to all people and give everyone around me the power to define my worth, then I am diminishing my integrity. My self-worth and significance needs to be fulfilled in the person of Jesus Christ. I need to recognize that it is *who He is* that allows me to be who I am. When I am reflecting Him in my life, I am fulfilling His plan for me.

So that's *who* makes me significant. But *how* do we achieve true significance?

The most humbling part about a relationship with Christ is that it's not based on what we do or how well we do it. It is rather based upon our simple belief in Him. That's why Scripture says we need to have the faith of a little child.

Think of the kind of people who surrounded the Lord Jesus during the latter days of His earthly ministry. The scribes and teachers of the law were posturing and strutting their knowledge, their righteous performance, and their flashy Hebrew credentials. The Pharisees made sure everyone knew how important *they* were by the way they dressed, by their public praying and giving, and by the deference and respect they demanded from anyone less holy than they (in other words, the rest of humanity). Even the Lord's own disciples nursed visions of future greatness and argued among themselves over who would be minister of what in the soon-coming messianic kingdom.

About that time the Lord Jesus gave them all a little object lesson they would never forget.

He called a little child and had him stand among them. And he said: "I tell you the truth, unless you change and become like little children, you will never enter the kingdom of heaven. Therefore, whoever humbles himself like this little child is the greatest in the kingdom of heaven. And whoever welcomes a little child like this in my name, welcomes me." (Matthew 18:3-4)

The gospel writer Mark adds that Jesus took the child in His arms and embraced him.

It was as if the Lord was saying, "Listen guys. I know all about your impressive titles and degrees. I know all about your money and investments, your big-time reputations, and the exclusive designer labels on the inside of your robes. I know how you've scrambled to the top of the heap and how people bow and scrape and step out of the way when you come walking down the street. But let me tell you something. This little guy in My arms here—yes, this chubby, curly headed little guy with dimples—is way ahead of you. Look at him! He ran willingly into My arms. He came to Me, hurried right into My presence, with no pretensions, no agenda, no résumé, no hidden motives. He's content just to lean back into the arms of Christ and trust Me with all his heart. He's found the source of significance, and nothing he will do for the rest of his life will give him any more than he has right now. And as far as the kingdom of heaven is concerned, he's so far ahead of you, I don't see how you'll ever catch up."

Boy, didn't that set them back on their heels! A *kid?* A runny-nosed *child* greater and more significant than *me?*

That's right. Because the bottom-line question in God's eternal kingdom is not who you are, but *whose* you are.

It's not what you have, but who has you.

It's not what you've accomplished, but what Jesus has accomplished on your behalf.

It's not the praise and admiration of men, but the grace and acceptance of God.

It's not what you've acquired, but what you've surrendered.

You and I don't have to perform to be accepted. He accepts us with our flaws. It's *because* of our flaws and our inability to hit the mark that God sent His Son to die for us. Yes, He wants us to do well to bring honor to Him, but our relationship is sealed by a relationship, not a performance. The *how* part of our significance is answered by our simple acceptance of Him and His role in our life as Lord.

How long has it been since you've tossed aside all the heavy stuff you've been dealing with and just ran open-handed into His arms?

Finally, *what* does it mean to enjoy true significance? This is centered in the realization that we have a roadmap, both for our temporal life and eternal life with God. What if you were given the option to have either of two roadmaps: one showing how to make it through the trials, temptations, and struggles of life on earth, or another giving you the path to eternal life?

Fortunately, we don't have to choose. God gives us both!

He gives us both roadmaps with His Word, fellowship with other believers, and communication with Him through prayer.

Sounds too simple doesn't it? Most real truth is.

Welcome to significance, men.

Guard the truth…and guard your heart as well.

Application Suggestions:

1. In the past three years, who have you been trying hardest to please in your life? Make a list of the different possibilities (include yourself, God, and the names of others) to help you consider carefully your answer. Circle the name on the list that represents your most honest answer.

2. Write out your own personal definition of success. Begin this way: "I will be successful when…"

3. On the same sheet of paper, write out your own personal definition of significance. Begin this way: "I am significant because…" Decide where you can keep this sheet of paper so you can look often at your definitions of success and significance.

4. Remember the Philippians 4 pattern—*PRAYING thoroughly and with thanksgiving about everything… experiencing the PEACE of God… being GUARDED IN HEART and mind in Christ Jesus.* Write out a prayer to God that sincerely expresses your desire for finding your significance in Him alone.

To Think About & Discuss:

1. In his section "A Value Shift to Significance," the author quotes Galatians 1:10. Read this verse again and discuss these two questions: *In what ways am I (still) trying to gain significance through what others think about me?* and, *How can I shift to a posture of pleasing God rather than men?*

2. In 2 Chronicles 26:3-8, read about a king who enjoyed great success. What does verse 5 say about the secret of Uzziah's success? How did this success also reflect the deeper roots of significance?

3. Joshua 1:1-9 is another passage that speaks about *God-given* success (as opposed to shallow, temporary, "self-generated" success). What principles did the Lord give to his frightened servant (and to us) to ensure that success?

4. What did the self-absorbed, self-exalting disciples learn about true significance from Christ's "object lesson" in Matthew 18:3-4?

....

CHAPTER TEN

SNEAK ATTACK #2:
PASSIVITY

■

Name a famous venture that started out as a high risk gamble, flourished for a year and a half, then ended abruptly in disaster.

Some of you think I'm talking about a celebrity marriage. Others had flashbacks of some big business endeavor. Wrong on both counts. I'm talking a very thin slice of history that has captured America's imagination for more than a century...the Pony Express.

Here are the actual words of a recruitment poster:

PONY EXPRESS
St. Joseph, Missouri, to California
in 10 days or less.
—WANTED—
Young, Skinny, Wiry, Fellows not over eighteen.
Must be expert riders, willing to risk death daily.
Orphans preferred. Wages $25 per week.
Apply Pony Express Stables
St. Joseph, Missouri

Can't you see some young guys meandering up to those posters, thumbs hooked in their front pockets, hats tipped back on their heads, chewing wads of tobacco and looking each other in the eye with that "there's no way *you* could handle it, but *I* can" look.

It may have been the fastest way to get mail to the West Coast, but it wasn't cheap! The postage rate was as high as $10 an ounce. The mail was lost only once in the 650,000 miles ridden by the Express. It was definitely the way to go, "when it absolutely, positively, had to be there in ten days."

The Old West—it was a time and a place riddled with social ills, disease, and hardship. But when you plop in your Lazy Boy, sit back with a bowl of buttered popcorn and a Diet Coke, and start channel surfing with your remote, there's nothing quite like losing yourself in a good Western.

Hey, those were the days. When men were men and women were women and horses were horses and kids were kids. Speaking of kids, where are they when you need 'em? You could use another Coke from the refrigerator.

From the Pony Express to the couch.

Seems like we've lost something in the intervening years, doesn't it?

What has happened to men in our culture today? When did men become so passive? When did men become content to watch so much of the action, instead of being a part of it? As I've counseled with scores of couples over the years, it's become clear that a husband's passivity is one of a wife's most profound dreads.

He's here, but he's not here.

He's three feet away, but a light year out in space.

The light's on, but no one's home.

Been there? I have. It's as if we fray so many neurons in our brain during the workday that we have nothing left over when we come home.

Understandable? You bet. Trouble is, there's someone—or a group of someones—waiting and waiting for you—all of you—to walk through that front door.

- A fuzzy headed little baby who knows who Daddy is, but can't say the word yet.
- A thirsty and responsive woman who has shouldered her own heavy load during the day.

- An elementary aged son, who asks one more time, "Dad, can we play catch tonight? Just for a few minutes?"
- A high schooler who doesn't ask quite so often, but you realize in your heart of hearts that the clock is ticking and you're in the eighth inning of the active parenting years.
- An adult daughter or son who would walk across America with no shoes on to hear you say, "Honey, I'm proud of you." Or, "Son, you're doing a great job. Keep it up!"

Why do so many of us forget how to kick out of our inertia as husbands and dads and kick into the groove with our families? Why is it that as Barbara and I speak across this country, the number one thing women tell us is that they're scared, frustrated, and fed up with the passivity of their husbands? Why does a man who stood in a wedding ceremony before many witnesses and promised to take the steering wheel end up snoozing in the back seat as the years go by? Why are men becoming increasingly passive when the times are becoming more demanding, both in our homes and culture?

I want to talk about passivity in this chapter. I want to confront our inclination to back off when it's clear that being active—and even proactive—is really the best call. How did we get to this point? What happened? And what do we do now?

The Roots of a Passive Generation

Many of us men try to shift the blame to our wives, complaining about their shouldering in and taking control of things. And in many marriages that's a legitimate issue. But it isn't the core issue. The core lies with us. If and when they do step to one side, you and I don't step up to the plate.

Some say that masculine leadership in the home began to change with the advent of World War Two...the Big One. There may be some truth in that theory, but I'm not sure if the big war started the problem or only *accelerated* it. We know that children in the home were more influenced by their dads before the war than after it. Following the war, many men moved from agricultural jobs to the factories. Others hit the road as traveling salesmen or punched a clock as clerks and office workers. This was an unprecedented change in our culture. And when the men moved from family farms and home-based businesses, the families went through a revolution of change.

Dads who just a few years before were working alongside their own fathers now found themselves separated from their own families by their jobs. Interaction time with wife and kids began to evaporate. That's about the same time most of us baby boomers entered the world. For many of us growing up in the fifties and sixties, our father was absent from our lives for the major part of our childhood. We may not have had the role model we needed to help us learn what it means to be a man at home. So the reason we don't assume leadership may be simply because we don't know how.

I know a lot of men all across this country who want to lead. They don't want to be passive. They want to step into their rightful role in the home. But the combination of lack of training, conflict with their wife, distractions, and other "threats to their castle" keep them frozen with anxiety or weary to the point of apathy. The resulting passivity is eroding homes, eroding men's self-confidence, and eroding healthy marriages.

Why do we slip into this passive mode?

How Passivity Takes Over

Let's consider seven possibilities.

1. You may be passive because of your reaction to your wife.

This isn't about blame, just explanation. It may not have even started with your generation. Your dad may have been passive because of his reaction to his wife, your mother. Perhaps your mother or your wife grew up in a home where a dad overpowered the others in the family. She reacted by pledging to never experience that type of pain again. So she took the bull by the horns and became dominant and controlling. From her perspective, it was "control or be controlled."

If your mother took this role, your dad may have sold out to her in order to keep the peace. He may have turned family leadership over to her, retreating to a safe zone of work, hobbies, or sports. You name it, it happens in families. You may be repeating this pattern in your own home. It may be tough truth to swallow, but you may have married a woman like your controlling mother in order to be taken care of and dominated.

2. Passive males may be the only kind your wife knows.

Perhaps your mother or wife grew up in a home where the father was absent, distant, or passive himself. The woman *had* to take the lead, if only to keep the rudderless ship from drifting into the rocks. As a consequence she may have developed a strong personality, determined to keep up the walls of self-protection in her marriage. In response to her "control," you pull out and let her run the show.

3. Men become passive because they're short-distance runners.

We read a book, hear a sermon, or go to a men's conference and realize we need to make a fresh commitment of energy and focus to our family. It's a good resolution, and we really mean it. We square our shoulders, hitch up our britches, and make a few changes. We may go to a counselor once or twice, engage our kids in a talk, get involved in discipline, or launch some new family-improvement campaign. But then, when we don't see miraculous results in thirty-six hours, we tend to give up and crawl back into our passivity.

Maybe you feel I'm being a little harsh. I don't intend to be harsh, just direct. The greatest problem with short-distance fathering is that we tend to raise sons and daughters who develop difficulty trusting. When we develop a pattern of in-and-out parenting, our kids learn something: We're inconsistent. Yes, we're all inconsistent, to a degree. I know I am. But when we take repeated, impulsive leaps into active fathering—and then neglect to follow through, it breaks hearts in our family. Initially, it just hurts. Later on, it embitters.

- "Son, this weekend I'm going to take you fishing. I promise."
- "Honey, let's talk after school about your fight with Melinda. I have to head off to work right now. But it's a date. Be there."
- "I really wanted to come by and get you last night for dinner. I just got busy at the office."

Maybe you've uttered phrases like these. Maybe you heard them growing up. These are the well-intentioned words of dads who failed to follow through. And after a while, those pronouncements begin to fall on deaf ears.

Yes, it's true you have to "start somewhere," and these short bursts of energy do get the ball rolling. *But follow through.* For the sake of your family, get into the trenches, get someone to hold you accountable, and stay on course to build the trust of your kids. Kids need to trust their dads, or their world feels shaky and insecure. Some of you have only to look back on the relationship with your own dads to affirm this truth.

4. Some men are passive because they haven't resolved conflict.

Some of us men are wounded and hurt. We don't trust easily, we self-protect, we pull away from intimacy in relationships. We carry the wounds and scars of past hurts. We become hostile or passive to get back at those who've hurt us. Does it work? Oh yeah…but it also kills the hearts of those desiring a relationship with us.

5. We may be passive because we're just plain lazy.

Now there's a novel thought. And not a very pleasant one, either. Yet it's true. When we think about walking up to the Pony Express poster and casting our lot as a long-distance horseman, we end up settling for a long-distance nap. If we were to be gut-level honest, we may be unmotivated, selfish, and unwilling to give family leadership a fair shot.

The hard truth is that indifference and laziness can erode a marriage faster than anything. In some ways, it's easier for a woman to face a harsh verbal fight with her man than watch him withdraw into silent, preoccupied passivity. It leads her to say, "What happened? He had so much hope and vision. He wanted to make a difference. And I believed in him. But I just don't know anymore."

6. Many men are passive because they confuse "leadership" with "control."

Here's the scene: A guy knows in his gut that he's been out of touch with his wife and kids for way too long. So, as we described earlier, he gives fathering a short energy burst. Straight out of the blue, he comes charging onto the scene in a general's uniform, suddenly barking orders and laying down the law. His bewildered family asks, *What's this all about? What got into him?* When they don't immediately toe the line and start marching in his parade, this dad gets discouraged and disgusted, and beats a retreat back into isolation and passivity. "Hey," he mutters, "I tried, but nobody listened." And his wife may be heard muttering, "You call *that* leadership? I call it a frustrated power play."

7. Some men are passive because that's all they know.

If we've never seen a model of a plugged-in, fully engaged husband and dad, we may simply not know how it's done. It's like trying to speak a foreign language. That's where good books on male leadership can begin to fill a vacuum in our lives. (Two of the best are by two of my favorite people. Get your hands on *Point Man* by Steve Farrar and *Tender Warrior* by Stu Weber.)

Breaking the Pattern

Does any of this stuff hit home? Do you see any old patterns passed along from your dad and his dad now making an appearance in *your* home? Let's break out of this tiresome rut! Don't be discouraged. Just realize where things stand and begin to do something about it.

This is one of those sneak attacks against our castle, remember? This is one of the ways that our wily enemy wants to get inside the walls of our hearts and homes and haul down our banner from the flagpole.

That's okay. That's why we have this book about guarding your heart. We're going to get after it together, and get the job done.

Here are five ideas to help us take the offensive and hit this sneak attack head on.

1. Recognize God's design for you as a man.

People like to try to obscure or complicate the issue, but the biblical mandate for men is really plain and simple. We're called to be the leaders of our home. In Genesis 2:18, the Lord said, "It is not good for the man to be alone. I will make a helper suitable for him." The fashioning of Eve to be Adam's helper was God's way of allowing man and woman to mutually complete each other. God's plan of making woman the helper was not putting the woman in a "one down" position. To the contrary, it's a word that places the woman in high esteem. The Hebrew word translated as "helper" is equivalent to the English word "completer," and it's used most often in the Old Testament of God Himself. It's a title of honor and worth.

In the New Testament, the apostle Paul spells it out like this:

> For the husband is the head of the wife as Christ is the head of the church, his body, of which he is the Savior. Now as the church submits to Christ, so also wives should submit to their husbands in everything.
>
> Husbands, love your wives, just as Christ loved the church and gave himself up for her to make her holy, cleansing her by the washing with water through the word, and to present her to himself as a radiant church without stain or wrinkle or any other blemish, but holy and blameless. In this same way, husbands ought to love their wives as their own bodies. He who loves his wife loves himself. After all, no one ever hated his own body, but he feeds and cares for it, just as Christ does the church, for we are members of his body. (Ephesians 5:23-30)

Direct? You bet. It's pretty hard to back off God's intention for us. We may not want the role, we may not feel we're very good at it, but beyond question, it is God's design for our lives.

So what does it mean to be the head? Does it mean we hold control over our wives? Does it mean we dominate and put our wives in their place?

Headship is not about domination or worth or power. Headship is about *responsibility.* We are responsible to lead our homes by serving our wives, just as Christ serves the church. He didn't beat the church into submission. He didn't threaten it or bully it or try to intimidate it. No, He continually loves and serves the church, to the point of yielding His very life.

But in a real sense our wives do need to be "in their place," that is, in a role of respecting us and submitting to us. But we men must set the pace! It is *our* attitude, behavior, and belief about submission that sets the pace for how our wives relate to us.

The bottom line: If I'm leading Barbara by serving her and loving her, it will make her submission to me acceptable and reasonable. But for this to work, she needs to see me actively engaged in my role as leader of the home. When I am active and when she observes me submitting my heart to Christ, she feels more secure in placing herself under my protection. Yes, there have been distortions and weird caricatures of this relationship for generations. But when we attempt to live out the roles of husband and wife as God actually designed them —leaning on Him for strength and wisdom—marriage really *works*.

2. Count the hours you have with your kids.

My friend Jerry Wunder has three daughters. Realizing how quickly they were growing up, he recently sat down with his calculator and computed the number of days he had left with each of them before high school graduation and departure for college. He then calculated the number of hours he could increase his exposure to them if he went home from work one hour earlier each day. After completing his calculations, he went to his office, opened his calendar, coldly slashed out the last hour of each business day, and went home.

Just like that.

When Jerry told me about this approach, I sensed the Holy Spirit delivering a message straight from Jerry's heart to my own. I was convicted on the spot. The next Monday I met with my office staff and made the same adjustment. I still recall my secretary's comment: "You can't do that, Gary—all your clients want those five o'clock appointments." I did it anyway.

Yes, our family finances took a hit. We felt it, and it hurt. But it wasn't as big a hit as my family was taking in my absence. Besides, it made me a hero! Barbara loved it, my kids got to see their dad, and I ended up less brain-dead than before. Are there exceptions? Sure, sometimes I can't pull it off. But most of the time I do.

By the way, if my calculations are correct, as of this moment, I have increased the number of hours with my high school sophomore, Sarah, by 1,030 hours. With my seventh grader, Missy, I've picked up an extra 2,125 hours.

My clients can get another counselor. I just don't want my kids to have another dad. They have a dad.

3. If passivity is an issue, confess it and move in another direction.

Repent is a good old word that's been out of fashion for a long time. Maybe it needs to make a reappearance. What the word actually means is to *change your mind.* It means that as you're going in one direction you stop, turn around, and start going in another direction.

When we as men are struggling with something—anything—in our lives, we need to confess it and receive God's forgiveness. Passivity is one of those things, isn't it? In Psalm 32:5 we read, "Then I acknowledged my sin to you and did not cover up my iniquity. I said, 'I will confess my transgressions to the Lord' and you forgave the guilt of my sin."

If you are being passive and want to step back into the role God designed for you, then realize that it begins with acknowledging your shortfall to Him, accepting the forgiveness that only God can give, and getting back in the saddle.

But it doesn't stop with confessing to God.

It also helps to go to a brother, as a second step. James 5:16 tells us, "Therefore, confess your sins to each other and pray for each other so that you may be healed. The prayer of a righteous man is powerful and effective."

That's a potent word of encouragement, isn't it? We need to confess it to a brother, a man who is willing to listen and then to encourage us to follow through and stick close to the Lord, our power source.

Next step? Go to your wife, and do the same with her.

You may want to invert that order—going first to your wife and second to the friend. It's your call. Just be cautious not to violate any confidentiality of your marriage bond by sharing something in a way that could offend your wife.

Ask God for directions in these sensitive areas. He'll come through for you.

4. Communicate to your wife your intention of taking the lead.

Let her know you want to take a shot at leading and being increasingly active in your marriage and family. Tell her what you need from her. Maybe it's to plan with you an incremental approach to stepping back into your marriage. Start small. Realize that you won't be capable of jumping into this full speed any more than you could jump into being a marathoner. Getting in shape to run the Boston Marathon begins with a first step. So does moving into a leadership role in your home.

Where do you start? What does a first step look like?

Maybe it starts by coming home an hour earlier every day, like my friend Jerry did.

Maybe it starts with conserving enough energy to give your wife fifteen to twenty minutes of meaningful conversation each night, telling her about your day and listening as she tells you about hers.

Maybe it starts with taking your bride out for a date. Like old times, right? On a Friday night you go out for a piece of pie, and talk about your love for her, your dreams of the rest of your life together, and the desire of your heart to be the man God wants you to be.

Whatever the needs are, communicate them to your wife. You don't have to be an expert, just willing to try. Take the risk. Your relationship is worth it.

5. Find a man or group of men to team up with for mutual encouragement.

Who do you know out there who's doing this marriage thing right? Why don't you buy him breakfast some time and get some good feedback on the best ways to impact your wife and kids? It would be honoring to him, the Lord, and also your family if you took the risk to allow someone an inside look at some of your thoughts, struggles, and needs. Saddle up with a group of guys once a week, read a good book on the role of men who have a heart for their families, and commit to praying for each other.

It really boils down to a simple point: We were designed to lead, our wives were designed to follow.

It's God's plan.

It's right.

And it starts by getting off the couch, checking out the job description on the Pony Express poster, and saddling up. While you're at it, give that TV clicker a toss. Pretend you're George Washington tossing a silver dollar across the Potomac, and let that thing sail.

Your favorite pro team will never notice your absence.

But your family will never win without you.

Application Suggestions:

1. Take a pencil and paper (or a calculator). Based on the current ages of your children and the number of years you have left with them before they leave home, how much additional time could you spend with them if you had one more hour available each workday? How does that measure against whatever you would give up by missing that hour at work? Make a decision soon about whether to take off one hour earlier from work each day in order to be with your children.

2. Write down your own evaluation of how well you are leading your home. Then decide on a time and a place to ask your wife to evaluate how well you are leading your home.

To Think About & Discuss:

1. Consider Paul's strong encouragement to believers in Romans 12:9-12. There are at least ten commands in these three short verses. Identify how obeying each one—as you allow the life of Christ to empower you—can work against passivity in your home.

2. Going back to verse 11 in the above passage, describe what the description "lacking in zeal" looks like when applied to a husband and father? What does "spiritual fervor" look like? How can Paul's commands in verses 1 and 2 of chapter 12 help us move from the first description to the second?

3. The author asks, "When did men become content to watch so much of the action, instead of being a part of it?" Another way of saying this might be, "If Satan can't make us fall, he'll put us to sleep." Carefully identify and consider the "action steps" laid out for husbands and dads in the following Scriptures. How could being accountable to a small group of like-minded brothers help us to shake off passivity in each of these areas?
Deuteronomy 4:9-10 and 6:4-8; Proverbs 13:24, 19:18, 23:13, and 29:17; 1 Thessalonians 2:11-12; Ephesians 5:25-29, and 6:4.

4. Since we men are instructed to love our wives "as Christ loved the church," our love needs to be modeled and patterned after His. How *active* is His love for us? What would life be like if Christ's love toward us was sleepy and passive?

CHAPTER ELEVEN

SNEAK ATTACK #3:
CONTROL

■

Our culture celebrates people who wield power and control.

We make them into heroes.

On the screen, in the ball parks, in the capital, in the magazines; from Trump to Turner, from Knight to Ditka, from Madonna to Nicholson; from tycoons to entertainers, from coaches who run teams with iron fists to politicians who bring shame to our government. One element seems to run true throughout the positions, the arenas, the spheres of influence.

Control.

Control has been bringing ruin to cultures, reputations, and relationships since the beginning of time. The rising stars of today and yesterday have fallen when the lights got too bright, the adulation too great, the control too tempting.

We've been on both sides of this one, haven't we? We've controlled others and in turn been controlled by others.

Control takes many different forms. It may be exerted through persuasion, manipulation, projection of guilt, expression of shame, or through withdrawal. Some men grew up in homes where control was habitually used. You may have had a dad who controlled you by his disapproval, a mom who controlled you through guilt, a brother who controlled you by half nelsons, and a sister who controlled you with the lashing of her tongue. A grandparent may have put the hammer down by criticizing, an aunt by shaming, and an uncle by belittling.

Control. It happens on all fronts and men mark it as one of the biggest issues they deal with. Whether it's a boss, a wife, a rebellious teen, an angry parent, or a passive colleague, control plays havoc in your life.

Make no mistake about it, we've all been controlled by others and when we are, it squashes our spirit. We may not know it right at the time, but we figure it out later. And when we do, it smarts. By the same token, we've all used control techniques in our relationships with others. Here's what it looks like.

The Four Faces of Control

After many discussions with men on this issue, both in the counseling office as well as in my speaking ministry and CrossTrainers, I came up with what I believe are the four faces of control: fear, deep insecurity, active or passive aggression, and lack of self-esteem.

Face #1: Fear

You may have grown up in a home or live in one now where control was exercised through fear. Fear that you didn't measure up. Fear of the rage that was about to engulf you if you didn't successfully navigate the emotional minefields. Fear that if you didn't toe the line—whatever arbitrary line it happened to be— you wouldn't be safe. You could be hurt or humiliated. Intimidation was the name of the game. And like all fear, it was wounding.

The wounding may have been verbal, emotional, physical, and even sexual. Your father or mother may have raged, drunk, beat, berated, criticized—pick your poison. Maybe you drank that poison, and maybe you're spooning it out to your kids even now. But poison is poison and it needs to be purged from our lives.

How do men from these homes cope? They tend to wrap themselves in layer upon layer of self-protection, allowing no one to get close to them. They never feel like they measure up. They look around them at other men who seem to enjoy intimacy with their wives, children, and friends, and ache for that type of closeness. But even if someone does reach out to them in friendship, they may very well sabotage the effort because they've learned that they don't deserve relationship and closeness. Too many tapes play over and over in their own heads, telling them how worthless they are.

Let's take a moment to consider a man who exercises a great deal of control. Control over business holdings, a television network, a baseball team, and even the reporting of the news. His face is familiar. He's known for his accomplishments, holdings, and power.

His name is Ted Turner.

Turner seems to have a strong and controlling way about him. Where does this insatiable drive to accumulate come from? Did he just happen on this trait in the midst of his career, or are the roots a bit deeper? I've read about him to try to gain an understanding of who he is and what might feed his pursuits in the world of gain and acquisition.

You don't have to look too hard or too deep before you run across some major trauma. One point of view says Turner carries a deep fear that he will end up the way his own father did: dead by suicide. The writer (in *Time* magazine, January 6, 1992) goes on with his speculations:

> It is also possible to see Turner's global pursuits as an elaborate attempt to heal from the first two traumas of his life. When he was twenty and she was three years younger, his sister, Mary Jane, died of a severe form of lupus erythematosus, a disease that causes the body to make antibodies against its own tissues. Until he saw her degenerate during five horrible years, Turner had been a practicing Christian. At seventeen he even planned to be a missionary. But the loss of his sister killed his faith in God. While Turner never recovered that faith, he has found a way to recover his proselytizing impulses as an apostle of peace and preservation. "It's almost like a religious fervor," he says.

What drives a man like Ted Turner? Is it his avoidance of dealing with the pain of the two significant losses of his father and sister? Could a man like Turner who has everything the world has to offer be driven by his fear of repeating his dad's legacy of self-destruction? I don't know him, so it's hard to say, but I don't think his life story is a lot different from many men I've encountered in counseling. When we lose someone as significant as a family member, we're gripped by an incredible sense of loss. We need to grieve that loss. To take the time to process it through. Some do, but others stuff the grief into a back closet of their soul. Control is one of the mechanisms people choose to cope with the pain and keep that closet door closed and locked.

Fear that isn't dealt with will often manifest itself in controlling behaviors. The acquisition of power, domination, and possessions are all short term fixes for a long term pain.

"Well," you may say, "I'd *take* a little of that fear if I could have Ted Turner's bank account." That's one way to look at it. But I choose a different slant. It makes me wonder if the Teds of the world would gladly take our place and give up their holdings to be released from a gnawing, ceaseless, debilitating *fear*.

Regardless of the size of our bank accounts or stock portfolios, we all have to put our heads on a pillow at night and do a review of our day. If you find that fear is seeping out from under the door of some inner closet, leading you to act in a controlling manner, then meet that fear with a powerful word from God. It is He who instructs us to replace that fear with another powerful motivator...*love*.

> There is no fear in love. But perfect love drives out fear, because fear has to do with punishment. The one who fears is not made perfect in love. We love because he first loved us. (1 John 4:18-19)

Face #2: Insecurity

Another face of control is deep insecurity.

Sometimes we control others because we feel it's the only way to deal with our own insecurity. A man who exhibits this kind of insecurity may never feel safe, even in his own home. As a child, he may have been smothered by the control of a parent, so he may dominate others in order to feel safe. Taking the risk to let his wife or kids have responsibility is to risk losing the very control he thinks he needs in order to survive. He sees allowing others to grow and experience life, make decisions, and expand their own boundaries as a threat to him. So due to his insecurity, he turns the heat up and kicks into a domination role.

What do those around him experience? Hurt, pain, anger, frustration.

When a man is deeply insecure, it's as if someone has punched a hole in his heart. No matter how much love, attention, and affirmation you pour into him, his heart leaks. So he continues to make demands on others to fill the emptiness he feels inside. Yet because he never fills up, the cycle continues. He demands; others try to measure up by giving; he is never satisfied; the home is in pain. When we are so deeply insecure, a new job, car, wife, or toy is not going to fill the void.

Only a transcending relationship can do that. A relationship with Jesus Christ.

Power, possessions, people, and travel are all short-term fixes; they can't satisfy. They're fun and glitzy, but they don't last. But we keep on searching, possessing, and trying to meet our insecurity needs in short yardage ways. And the cost is high. Because often the cost is that of relationships: with God, and with those who love us and need us.

Face #3: Aggression, both active and passive

Perhaps the easiest face of control to peg is active aggression. There's another type I'll address in a few moments, but let's look at the active, explosive type first. It's loaded with emotion, red faces, loud voices, and sharp comments. It is anger out of control, like a city in grave danger:

> Like a city whose walls are broken down
>   is a man who lacks self-control. (Proverbs 25:28)

It's throwing up our hands. It's barking and howling. It's threats. It's scowls. Aggression is an acting out of our hurt in a way that wounds others. It's control being exercised in the most demanding ways. It frightens others, leads them to feel threatened, and destabilizes homes.

One well-known sports figure illustrates this kind of aggression. Mike Ditka's history as a coach, player, and celebrity has been well documented. Memories of him reaming out quarterbacks and officials are etched in memory. But what about the impact of his emotional outbursts and struggle for control on his own family?

After interviewing her friends the Ditkas, Jeannie Morris said this (as reported in *Ditka: Monster of the Midway):*

> The Ditka marriage [to Marge], like many others of that time, was dysfunctional from the start. I don't think it was ever any good. Mike and Marge, I mean, you can put it in a nutshell. Mike and Marge never got along...You know, I think the deal was that when they got married, they got married with the idea of being married forever. I mean, there was nobody else he wanted to marry and he thought he was supposed to get married. Both are very strong willed and they're very much alike, and Marge tried to go by the rules for a long, long time...The rules being he's the boss and we do everything his way, and if he doesn't feel like being here for whatever period of time he doesn't have to be.

Megan Ditka, his daughter, is twenty-nine now and reported to the author of *Ditka: Monster of the Midway:*

> I have very few recollections of my father. My mom basically raised us by herself. I love my mom a lot. She's a real brave woman. I couldn't ask for anybody better. My dad was never really around a lot. And even when he was, he wasn't. We were always pretty much afraid of my dad. My dad is just like his dad. You didn't have conversations with him. He's a little intimidating when you're a kid...I don't think he knows how to love."

I don't know the private Mike Ditka. But it's clear that his drive to succeed, his focus, and his strong emotions impacted his family and cost him dearly.

Enough on the actively aggressive type. What about the other type, the passive type of aggression?

The passive response is also a controlling mechanism, although of less high octane than the aggressive response. But it is still powerful and every bit as controlling. Men become passive when they feel out of control. This is called the passive response, nailing people even when they may not know that's what's happening. Sometimes we do it through our moods, other times our withdrawal, and other times by our silence.

Men become passive and withdraw when they're shaken. The stress in the home and the office may prompt a guy to withdraw and isolate himself. Men who act passively have unmet needs, unfulfilled expectations, and blocked desires. Rather than expressing their needs in an up-front way, they use control by avoiding the issues.

Many of us will pull out all the stops to avoid a conflict or confrontation. So we unplug from relationships and plug into what is safe. Plopping into an easy chair, downing a bag of pretzels and a couple Cokes, and unplugging from life may be the drug of choice. When men feel they aren't in control, one of the easiest responses is to shut down. We're under the misconception that if we're quiet and alone, we can't screw things up any worse.

Yet we know that our very absence can *add* to the problem. In order to deal with conflict, we need to be involved in the relationship. We need to "be there," actively dealing with the issue. Passive responses are controlling responses. Let's admit it and reach for a healthier response.

Withdrawing and avoiding is a controlling behavior indeed. It's hard to reason with someone who won't communicate with you. It leads others to feel impotent in dealing with the issues at hand.

Face #4: Low self-esteem

Combining fear with deep insecurity and aggression often results in low self-esteem. Self-esteem is simply our perception of "how God sees me."

We are often misunderstood all day by people in the marketplace. What many men long for is to be understood at home. It's just that we don't always ask for that understanding in a healthy and direct way. So often, our poor self-esteem gets acted out in a controlling manner.

When we return home at the end of the day, we're leaving the world where we feel connected, and entering our family's world. Often it's an alien world, a world filled with emotions, different stages of growth, conflicts, and needs. That's why when men are feeling stress, no matter how demanding our work is, we often find ourselves wanting to go back to the office. At least we know what that map looks like! And our self-esteem has a greater chance of being stroked there, even though it's typically short-lived and transient. Real self-esteem is established when we are connected to relationships that last: with our Lord, with our wife, and with the children God has given us.

The four faces of control. Fear, deep insecurity, aggression, and low self-esteem. Any one of them or combination of them will lead to pain. Join me in a look at a controller who not only had control as king, but a character flaw that would give him premier placement in the controller's hall of fame.

Portrait of a Controller

Jeroboam, whose story is recounted in 1 Kings 11–14, was a man who had serious problems with control. He didn't start that way, but when he suddenly found himself in a position of power, position, and money, his life story took a series of tragic wrong turns.

By the way, you and I don't have to take those same wrong turns! We don't have to smash our life and crash our family into the same brick walls. That's why a gracious God gave us a Bible full of character portraits, complete with warts, blemishes, body odor, and dirty little secrets. I love the way Paul puts it in his letter to the Romans:

> For everything that was written in the past was written to teach us,
> so that through endurance and the encouragement of the
> Scriptures we might have hope. (Romans 15:4)

When we read Jeroboam's story, God wants us to gain wisdom and choose a different route. Think of the heartache and frustration we could dodge if we spent more time in this matchless Book of books!

We first encounter Jeroboam in Scripture as a simple laborer doing repair work on the wall of Jerusalem. He was juggling bricks and slapping mortar when he was discovered by King Solomon. In today's culture it would be like when a pro scout sits in the stands and sees the future of his franchise out there on the college football field. He watches him stretch before the game, play his heart out, and cheer on the other guys. The scout fills up two sheets of notebook paper recording the play of a guy who can do it all...work hard, lead, follow, play, and command the respect of his teammates.

Solomon's discovery of Jeroboam was like that. This guy's work ethic was so impressive that Solomon gave him the responsibility of running the entire labor force. He put him in as the first string quarterback of his building project.

Quite a responsibility for a young man. For Jeroboam it was only the beginning.

Not much later, Jeroboam had an encounter with a prophet of the Lord. God's spokesman laid out a vision that would change Jeroboam's life forever. There are a couple of "boams" here, so stick with me. (Rehoboam was Solomon's son. Jeroboam was a contemporary of Rehoboam.) It was foretold that God would punish Solomon's foolish son, Rehoboam, by tearing his kingdom apart: giving ten tribes to Jeroboam and two to Rehoboam. The prophet also gave Jeroboam a direct message from the Lord Himself:

> However as for you, I will take you, and you will rule over all that your heart desires: you will be king over Israel. If you do whatever I command you and walk in my ways and do what is right in my eyes by keeping my statutes and commands as David my servant did, I will be with you. (1 Kings 11:37-38)

What a promise! It was better than winning the Jerusalem lottery. Though he had no experience and was no kin to royalty, Jeroboam was to be handed ten twelfths of the nation with just one hitch: that he remain obedient to God. When we are given much, much is expected. And with increasing responsibility the stakes get higher.

Apparently, after Solomon learned of the prophet's visit to Jeroboam, the old king tried to have his former employee assassinated. So Jeroboam became a man on the run. He fled to Egypt to save his skin, only to return after Solomon's death. With Solomon dead, events began to accelerate. Jeroboam returned from exile to challenge Rehoboam and his treatment of the people, asking for leniency rather than the heavy labor and tax burdens Solomon had placed upon the people. Most teams would love to follow a quarterback that went to the coach to ask for a reduction in a heavy practice schedule. What a way to build a following. It worked.

In his youth and immaturity, Rehoboam sought the counsel of his young friends rather than the counsel of the elders. His harsh rejection of the people's request played right into Jeroboam's hands.

The national split foretold by the prophet made Jeroboam king over all Israel—excepting the tribes of Judah and Benjamin. What a roller coaster ride for a young construction foreman! And it could have been the beginning of measureless, matchless, eternal glory for the young man if only…if only…if only.

Remember the *one requirement* laid on Jeroboam as he was being handed the keys to the shiny new northern kingdom? God simply asked him to be obedient. Period. But for Jeroboam, it was one requirement too many. He had his own agenda. He led his kingdom away from God almost immediately, knowing full well that God promised to judge him harshly if he did. Make any sense? Only if we're so gripped by the desire to control that we figure we know better than the Almighty.

As Jeroboam began to lead his people, he was suddenly afraid he might lose his grip on this heady new feeling of power. After all, if his subjects kept going down to Jerusalem to worship at the temple, they might get ideas about restoring the old kingdom. The solution? Keep them from worshiping the Lord! He quickly created two golden calves, shrines, and appointed "all sorts of people" as priests. There was no need for his people to make the pilgrimage to Jerusalem. He'd give them all the worship and ceremony they wanted right in good old Samaria.

Talk about control. Oh, how tightly he clung to those reins of power! His teeth were clenched and his knuckles were white. Now that he had the crown, he meant to keep every iota of authority. Not even God would interfere with his plan!

How utterly foolish. Who was it who gave him the opportunity in the first place? Who picked him up out of the construction crew and put him into that position of authority? Of course, it was God. The sovereign, all-powerful Yahweh of Israel. How could this young man possibly come to believe that he could maintain control apart from the God who gave him that control? Insanity!

If only Jeroboam had known God better. He would have relaxed. He would have smiled. He would have held the reins lightly. He would have realized that the God who places opportunity, position, and authority into a man's hand as a trust is the same God who can meet that man's every need. No need to fear! No need to scheme and connive and stay up late at night dreaming up this plan or that. No need to be tripped up by fear, insecurity, aggression, or low self-esteem. The wonderful, incredible secret to maintaining control is to yield that control back to God!

Is Jeroboam really any different than any of us? God is gracious with His blessings. He takes us in humble times and places incredible opportunities into our hands. He makes us husbands and dads and gives us authority in the church and on the job, asking only for our obedience. Yet so often we take His blessings and then rebel by trying to grab the controls of our life. We play stupid little games and try to control people and bully, coerce, or manipulate them into doing what we want them to do. Oh sure, we run to the Lord when we're hurting or needy. We seek Him *then*, But when life is rolling along, we tend to become increasingly self-reliant. The price of our own control? We find ourselves sitting in the ruins of an unraveling life moaning, "Oh God, why? Why me?" I think the more accurate question is "Why *not* me?"

Where Are You Controlling?

Let me ask you: Where are you controlling? Is it by pulling out of involvement in your family? Is it by being harsh? Dominant? Instead of yielding to the temptation to control and manipulate people and circumstances through hostilities or our moods, we need to surrender that control to Christ. Instead of being the pawn of controlling people, feeling as if we have to jump through hoops that keep getting higher and higher, we need to surrender the situation to Christ.

It's an incredible irony: We actually *gain* control of our lives by *yielding* control to Him. We trust Him to move people's hearts or change people and we tell it all to Him instead of trying to jump in there and do it all ourselves. Instead of controlling, men, be controlled… but only by God!

Those who live life by relying on themselves or well-practiced controlling techniques to get their own way and satisfy their own needs are living life without the power of the Holy Spirit. When you try to scheme, coerce, manipulate, connive—name your poison—the result will be a life of short-term gain at best and eternal loss. You may get what you want initially, but you will not get peace or happiness in the bargain.

Who said it better than the Lord Jesus Himself?

> Whoever find his life will lose it, and whoever loses his life for my sake will find it. (Matthew 19:39)

Let's lose a little control together, shall we? How about a lot of control? How about the whole shootin' match? How about letting Jesus Christ have it all?

Anyway you look at it, playing God is a pretty big role to master. And no one else comes near to matching *His* qualifications for it.

Application Suggestions:

1. Identify the method or manner by which you most often try to wrongly take control and rely on yourself instead of on God. Analyze the situations in which you are most tempted to do this. Ask yourself also, "What are the harmful effects of doing this?"

2. Recall again the Philippians 4 pattern—*PRAY thoroughly and with thanksgiving about everything… experience the PEACE of God… which will then GUARD YOUR HEART and mind in Christ Jesus.* Write out a prayer to God that sincerely expresses your desire to yield control of your life and family to Him.

To Think About & Discuss:

1. What do Matthew 20:25-28 and 2 Corinthians 1:24 have to say about the kind of control that "lords it over" others around us? How can we apply these verses to our roles as husbands and dads?

2. The author relates the story of Ted Turner who turned away from Christ after the agonizing death of his younger sister. To fill the aching void, the author suggests that Turner may have become obsessive in his need to drive himself and control various enterprises. How might the following passages have helped this man draw nearer to Christ in his grief instead of turning to "control"?
   Psalm 55:22, Matthew 10:28-29, John 7:37, and 1 Peter 5:7.

3. If fear and insecurity cause us to act in a controlling manner, how can the truth of 1 John 4:18-19 serve as an antidote?

4. Look again at the Lord's astonishing promise to Jeroboam in 1 Kings 11:37-38. What was God's path to authority and "control" for this young man? Name some of the amazing promises God has made to us as His redeemed sons. In what ways are we in danger of stumbling—like Jeroboam—over this issue of "control"?

CHAPTER TWELVE

SNEAK ATTACK #4:

COMPETITION

■

America's Team.

I never heard how the Dallas Cowboys came by that designation, but they have it and wear it with pride. Somehow, it seems to fit. For over twenty-nine years, the helm was captained by a gentleman. A gentleman who walked the sidelines sporting a gray suit and a brimmed hat. He was frequently stern-faced, but man, did he know how to win. The Cowboys captured two Super Bowl victories under his guidance, and played some of the finest football in the history of the NFL.

Tom Landry was the coach and the Cowboys were America's team. Landry has always been respected as a man of integrity and character, a man who put Christ first, not football.

Then one day in 1989, owner Jerry Jones decided to make a change.

The change was as different as black and white, chocolate and vanilla, east and west. Jones brought in Jimmy Johnson as the new coach, a college buddy and fellow football player. Things have never been quite the same in the big "D" since. The heart of Texas was now represented by a man who pulled out all the stops to lead the team to renewal, even though it took on a different personality. The new method of operation?

Competitiveness at all costs.

It's Part of Who We Are

Men compete. That competitive nature is simply a part of who we are. It's necessary to a large degree in order to protect our families, especially in a world like ours, that's becoming an increasingly hostile and dangerous place to live.

It began with toys, childhood games, and pick-up games of baseball and basketball. It used to be shooting baskets, now it's closing the deal before the other guy. We used to relish beating our brothers in a hot game of Monopoly, now it's getting a contract that every other guy in our field would drool over. Satisfaction as a kid was hitting the pillow after a day full of winning in anything we attempted. Today, for many, it's marked by the section of town we call home, the size of our financial portfolio, and the speed of our boat, car, jet ski, or motorcycle.

Competition.

Salesmen match monthly tallies. Doctors compare the number of patients they see in a day. Pastors go to ministerial meetings and ask, "And how many people do *you* have on Sundays?" We watch it on TV, fall back into it in our recreation, and live it on the highways. We don't even have to try to do it. It comes naturally. Men compete.

When Competition Goes Bad

Competition in and of itself is a plus, not a negative. It comes with the masculine territory. But what happens when it takes a destructive slant? What happens when that part of us that likes to jump off the bench and get into the game becomes a desire to do *anything* to beat the other guy? What happens when competition goes bad?

Remember the Texas cheerleader's mother? She was a mom who passionately desired to see her daughter win a spot on the high school cheerleading team. But something snapped under the weight and pressure of that overwhelming desire. She ended up hiring a hit man to take out her daughter's rival.

That's competition gone bad, folks. And it isn't limited to psychopathic mothers of cheerleaders. It also pervades the wide world of sports. Competition *within balance* is the very essence and core of the sporting world. Sometimes, however, that competition edges over the boundary lines.

A few years ago Texas Christian University played host to the University of Oregon football squad. The Horned Frogs taking on the Fighting Ducks. Quite a contest, huh? Sounds more like something you'd see on *Mutual of Omaha's Wild Kingdom*. Whatever the rest of the nation may have thought about it, the game certainly meant a great deal to the young men who were banging heads on the gridiron that Saturday afternoon. As it happens, the home team was getting beat up by the feisty Ducks. That was bad enough, but it was worse when the Frogs looked back over several seasons of humiliating football futility. For one offensive player on the bench, it was too much. As a fleet-footed Duck streaked down the sideline late in the game toward another sure touchdown, the frustrated Frog leaped *off the bench* and tackled him. It may have made him feel better for the moment, but it did nothing to help his team. The humiliation only deepened for his buddies, his coach, and his university.

Over in Cincinnati, consummate competitor Pete Rose had left the days of baseball glory behind him. But the dark side of his competitive drive still held him by the throat. As a member of the Reds organization, he was convicted of gambling on baseball games and brought shame to both America's pastime and the proud Reds tradition.

Competition within the rules is called "sport," but when we step over the line breaking the rules, it has another name.

It's called "war."

And the one thing that characterizes war is that it hurts and kills people. Even noncombatants. Even innocent women and children.

Pipo knows about the casualties of war. Just ask him. *Time* magazine did. And when I read the article ("A Sniper's Tale," March 14, 1994) I almost lost my lunch.

Pipo used to throw the javelin at track meets. At twenty-five years old and six-foot-three inches tall, he still could. But there isn't much need for javelin throwers where he lives today. Sarajevo doesn't look like the sporting town that housed the Winter Olympics only a few years ago. Today, it's a war zone, and Pipo plays in the game of life and death as a Bosnian sniper.

And Pipo is good at what he does. Very good.

His anger and keen marksmanship drew him to a sniper unit. From life as a fierce competitor to living life with ice in his veins, he is no longer the man he once was. He has become so comfortable on the other side of the line of competition that he doesn't feel anymore.

"I'm not sure I am normal anymore," he told the *Time* reporter. "I can talk to people, but if someone pushes me, I will kill them…In the beginning I was able to put my fear aside, and it was good. Then with the killing I was able to put my emotions aside, and it was good. But now they are gone. Everyone likes peace except me. I like the war."

It gets worse. Pipo keeps a tally of his "scores," but there isn't enough room left on his belt for all the notches. Pipo claims his bullets have downed 325 people. How does he handle the hardness of a heart that once competed with enthusiasm and now is afraid to feel? He learned a lesson from an officer, his sniper coach, who told him, "Don't let the faces follow you."

"I have no feelings for what I do," said the weary sniper. "I went to see my mother in Belgrade, and she hugged me and I felt nothing. It is our choice to go to hell…I have no life anymore. I go from day to day, but nothing means anything. I don't want a wife and children. I don't want to think." No, he says, not one of the faces he held in his sights was a civilian. But he makes the denial with a flat voice, eyes downcast. Any admission of firing at civilians could get him arrested and charged with a war crime.

You may read this and think, "Hey, that guy's six miles over the edge. He's lost the handle on his sanity. I could never step over the kind of lines Pipo has stepped over."

I know you wouldn't, friend. But if the sneak attack of competition is eroding your sense of what is right and fair, then what is crossing your own lines doing to you? Have you shut your eyes to the faces impacted by your competitive spirit that takes other people out? Are you so wrapped up in this normal masculine trait that you don't feel much anymore?

Competition without rules and balance hurts people. Let's take a closer look at how even "normal" competition in our lives can degenerate into an all-out warfare mentality that can destroy our castles and families.

Three Lethal Elements

What causes healthy competition to slide into something decidedly unhealthy? I think we can isolate three deadly elements. When these elements take over, competition mutates into something ugly, unstable, and even dangerous.

Lethal Element #1: Pride

Naaman was a proud man. Not the kind of bust-your-buttons pride you have in your kids when they excel, but the kind of pride that hardens hearts. As a hero and the commander of the army of the King of Aram, his courage and success mixed together gave him what my kids would call "an attitude." Scripture calls it a "proud heart."

He was not only a "valiant soldier" (2 Kings 5:1), but also suffered from a disease common to his day: leprosy. Of course he wanted to be healed of this loathsome condition, but in his pride he not only wanted to be healed, he wanted "preferential treatment." Pride has a way of giving people the illusion they "deserve" something extra in the attention department.

When he humbled himself to the degree of seeking a cure for his malady from the lowly king of Israel, General Naaman thought he'd come down plenty low enough. But the door to healing was much lower in the wall than the haughty commander was used to stooping. He couldn't walk upright through it, he couldn't bend just a little to go through it, and they surely didn't expect him to get down on his knees! Or…did they?

> So Naaman went with his horses and chariots and stopped at the door of Elisha's house. Elisha sent a messenger to say to him, "Go, wash yourself seven times in the Jordan, and your flesh will be restored and you will be cleansed."
>
> But Naaman went away angry and said, "I thought that he would at least come out to me and stand and call on the name of the LORD his God, wave his hand over the spot and cure me of my leprosy. Are not Abana and Pharpar, the rivers of Damascus,

better than any of the waters of Israel? Couldn't I wash in them and be cleansed?" So he turned and went off in a rage. (2 Kings 5:9-12)

Didn't these miserable Israelites know who he was? He was the great commander of a world-class army. He'd won huge, historic battles. He'd beaten down his competitors and was granted favor by God! And this so-called prophet wouldn't even give him the courtesy of meeting him at the door?

Elisha's instructions threw Naaman for a loop: It was humiliating to bathe in what he regarded as a small, dirty river. If he had to wash, he at least wanted to wash in a *great* river. He could maybe see himself standing out in the middle of some mighty current, leaning into the roaring white water with set jaw and a steely gaze. But dipping in that piddly little foreign stream?

Eventually, Naaman had to humble himself and obey Elisha's commands in order to be healed. He had to get down very low to find the door to healing…and the door to a relationship with the mighty God of Israel. A hardened heart had to be broken in order for Naaman to be healed.

"Before his downfall," Solomon wrote, "a man's heart is proud, but humility comes before honor" (Proverbs 18:12). Pride really does come before destruction. Whether we are a valiant soldier like Naaman or a hard driving businessman out to conquer our competitors, competition that breeds pride is lethal.

Make no mistake about it: if our heart is proud, a loving Father will correct us. He loves us enough to pull us back from the edge. He had to bring Naaman back to reality in order to reverse the lethal levels of pride in his own heart. The soldier who allowed his success to distort his perception of who he really was came up out of the Jordan River with new skin and a new attitude. When he obeyed, he was healed. Not only of his leprosy but also of a pride that would have eventually eaten away his life as surely as the disease.

Competition is good. It gets the blood boiling. But competition unchecked leads to pride. And pride unchecked leads to destruction.

How close are you to the line?

Lethal Element #2: Envy

Envy is looking at others and falling into the trap of wanting what they have. It may be their toys: boats, sports cars, big-screen TV, CD player, or whatever. It may be the people in their lives: their wife, their families, their friends. A jealous man is a perpetually unsatisfied and restless man. He is not content with God's provision. For him, contentment will always be just beyond reach.

Whenever I consider the subject of contentment, I start thinking about my car. My '85 Honda. I bought it new, almost ten years ago. When I got it, I was the envy of all the guys around me. It's that deep, metallic shade of dark blue— you've seen millions of them on the road. Every now and then I'll look down at that '85 Honda from my fifth floor office, and it looks pretty good. But the closer I get to it, the less attractive it is. The scratches, door dings, rust, worn tires, and other marks of wear and tear are pretty obvious from about ten feet.

But envy isn't known for looking at things up close, is it? Any of us can look good from far off. Proverbs 14:30 says, "A heart at peace gives life to the body, but envy rots the bones."

I was on an airline flight recently, and we were all standing in the aisle getting ready to deplane. Two guys were standing in front of me doing a little "envy talk" about their laptop computers. A businesswoman was standing between them as they kept one-upping each other. It was fun to watch her roll her eyes. She probably thought she was on the playground with two second graders, arguing about whose dad could beat up the other guy's dad.

"Hey, I see you have a new 486 DX with color screen. Passive or active?"

"Active, 200 megabyte."

You had to see it. They went back and forth for seven or eight minutes while the whole planeload of people listened on, comparing these machines that could land a man on the moon. Although neither of them would admit it, they probably each succeeded in making the other guy feel slightly less content with the computer draped over his shoulder.

What is contentment? When we're content, we're at peace. How does it feel? Some of you reading these words are experiencing that peace...like a drink of clear, cool water. It's as if you're kneeling over a mountain stream, cupping the water to your hands, and raising it to your mouth. You're in the high country of the Lord's presence and life is sweet. Others of you feel a long way from that quiet mountain top. You're in a valley that's dark and dry, and contentment seems like a distant fantasy. You're tired from continually looking over your shoulder at the accomplishments and possessions of other men.

Solomon tells us in Proverbs 4:25-27, "Let your eyes look straight ahead, fix your gaze directly before you. Make level paths for your feet, and take only ways that are firm. Do not swerve to the right or the left; keep your foot from evil."

Fix your gaze directly before you. Not on the other guy's stuff, power, possessions. Those are detours that will lead us to sin. Pride and envy start to form cataracts on our spiritual eyes, blinding us to the truth. God wants us to put aside anything that doesn't bring glory to Him. Use that as your plumbline. That's the plumbline I want in my life.

Lethal Element #3: Greed

> A greedy man brings trouble to his family,
> but he who hates bribes will live. (Proverbs 15:27)

When a man's competitiveness turns to greed, watch out. He's dangerous.

Remember the movie, "Wall Street," with Michael Douglas and his famous line, "Greed is good"? That's Wall Street's perspective. But greed, of course, isn't confined to Wall Street. It's alive and well everywhere.

Greed will distort our pursuit of God's plan for us. Paul writes in Colossians 3:5, "Put to death, therefore, whatever belongs to your earthly nature: sexual immorality, impurity, lust, evil desires *and greed*, which is idolatry." We need boundaries to protect us from these very aspects of the hardened heart. Greed is deadly to our walk in Christ.

Establishing the Boundary Lines

Every Saturday in the fall, hundreds of thousands of Americans walk into stadiums for an afternoon at the gridiron. Millions more sit in easy chairs to watch quick, agile, and very large young men play football on TV. High school kids play on Friday nights, the pros on Sunday afternoons. But regardless of the level of play there is one thing any football player knows: When they walk on that field, they're at war.

Guys get hammered, talk trash on the line, and sweat buckets. Blocks are thrown that would put me in traction for months. Ligaments are torn, bodies are tossed like the Sunday paper, and men beat on each other mercilessly. But there's one thing that's always true: Even these guys play by the rules. Why? Because they want to? Well, maybe. But they would likely try to win at all costs if there weren't a few older guys wearing black and white shirts running around on the field with whistles around their necks. These men in the striped shirts are called referees. They are in the game to make sure the other guys play fair.

So here's a question for you. Who plays the referee in your life? When competition goes from the games we play as kids to your career, friendships, and everyday lifestyle, who carries the whistle?

For some of you it's the Securities & Exchange Commission. On the work site, it may be OSHA. For others it's a licensing board. Maybe government watchdogs or private interest groups check your boundary lines to see if you've crossed them. Then for others it's just word of mouth on the street that leads you to stay inside the boundaries.

We all need boundaries. We need clear, unmistakable lines in the turf, placed there by a loving God to protect us from our own toxic levels of pride, envy, and greed. There is a balance that must be struck between *healthy competitiveness* and competition that has mutated into something unstable and sick. So why do so many men cross the boundary lines? For one reason, their competitive drive overtakes their sense of shooting straight and playing by the rules.

Let's do a little sports fantasy for a moment. Imagine yourself playing in a big game with your favorite college or pro football team. It's Saturday afternoon, umpteen thousands of fans are in the stands, and you're playing the game of your life.

In fact, it is the game of your *life story.*

Your wife and kids have seats halfway up on the fifty yard line. Your mom and dad are in a private sky box with your grandmother. Your pastor is over in Section 21B with a bunch of the guys from your men's group. It's game day and time for you to do your thing. You're fired up and ready because you've trained all your life for this day. You want to be the best you can be. To play hard and to play with courage, but most importantly, to stay within the lines. You don't want to win at all costs, because that would cheapen the victory. You want to win with honor. You want to compete in such a way that you can meet the eyes of your loved ones and savor their words: "I'm proud of you, son." "Honey, you were great out there." "Dad, you were awesome! Man, you played your heart out. I love you, Pop."

How do you do it? How do you stay in the lines when you know in your heart of hearts that a little move here and a slight shift over the line there could give you a short-term advantage—but might get you kicked out of the game? Here are *four boundary lines* for you to use when you're checking yourself out—or being checked out by someone who cares enough to hold you accountable. Imagine these four lines surrounding the four sides of your playing field, allowing you to compete with all your strength *within bounds*.

Boundary Line #1: Examine your motives

This one is within you. Motivation is something that lies below the waterline, down underneath a lot of the surface stuff. It's more revealing than our behaviors, attitudes, and even our thoughts. We can all try to do good things and think good thoughts. Even have good attitudes. But the acid test comes in when we ask ourself, "What's my motivation for doing what I'm doing? Is it pure?"

Paul tells us that the Lord will one day "bring to light what is hidden in darkness and will expose the motives of men's hearts. At that time each will receive his praise from God" (1 Corinthians 4:5).

- What is your motive for doing what you're doing on the job? Is it to make a living of honest gain and bring honor to God, or to build your own little prideful kingdom?
- Why are you seeking relationship with that particular person in your life? Is it clean, or when exposed to the light does it make you want to turn away in conviction?

- If you allowed God to examine your heart and search your motives (He has anyway), would He be pleased?

Direct hits? Then call a timeout and get some direction from the Coach. Clear the field, go back to the sidelines, and ask for a play that will put it in the end zone. One that will leave the whole crowd cheering and let you hold your head high.

Motives are close to the heart. They're real. It's good to do good things; it's better to do them out of pure motivations. God can use the boundary line of checking our motivations to keep our competition within boundaries...His boundaries.

Boundary Line #2: Listen to the Holy Spirit

You know that calm, insistent voice if you belong to Christ. It's the one that speaks to you when you lay your head on the pillow at night and review the activities of the day. It's a voice that speaks clearly, but doesn't shout. You have to slow down and quiet yourself to hear it. It's the voice that beckons you to obedience. The voice that probes your motivation.

Is it really "providing for your family" that's pushing you to sixty-hour work weeks?

Has pride replaced obedience as your goal in life?

Are you happy about Ron's success...or are you being eaten up with envy?

That was a big decision you just made. Was it based on a clean agenda?

Is your competitive drive edging out good judgment? Bringing out your dark side?

Jesus told His men:

> If you love me, you will obey what I command. And I will ask the Father, and he will give you another Counselor to be with you forever—the Spirit of truth. The world cannot accept him, because it neither sees him nor knows him. But you know Him, for he lives with you and will be in you. I will not leave you as orphans. (John 14:15-18)

I don't want to grieve the Holy Spirit. I don't think you want to, either. I want to leave a life story that will be a light for Jesus Christ so that others will be drawn to Him. We need to listen to that "still, small voice" of the Spirit when He speaks to us. He speaks because He loves us and wants us to receive His protection…within the boundary lines.

Boundary Line #3: Open your life to your friends

Men with power, money, and position can enjoy great successes in life. They can contribute much to others. But if they isolate themselves behind their castle walls and don't allow others to examine their hearts, they can also self destruct. Listen…*If you have successfully isolated yourself from examination by other brothers, you're on your way to your downfall.*

We need close brothers in our life. Not dozens of them, but a few good men. A few brothers who know our heart's desire. A little group of guys who won't buy our artful deceptions or flimsy excuses. Two or three men who have our number and the right to ask us uncomfortable questions. Not because they're nosy or super-critical, but because we've invited them to get in our faces. Listen to Paul's great wisdom about the importance of brothers willing to go the extra mile:

> Brothers, if someone is caught in a sin, you who are spiritual should restore him gently. But watch yourself, or you also may be tempted. Carry each other's burdens, and in this way you will fulfill the law of Christ. If anyone thinks he is something when he is nothing he deceives himself. Each one should test his own actions. Then he can take pride [the healthy kind] in himself, without comparing himself to somebody else, for each one should carry his own load. (Galatians 6:1-5)

What a good word for us as men today. When we're involved in a friend's life and we're seeing something that bothers us, we need to *gently* restore him. We also need to be cautious not to do this in a way that could lead us into sin ourselves. We need to love our friends enough to help them carry their burdens. We need to keep our self-perceptions in balance, and examine our *own* hearts so we don't fall into the trap of comparison. That's what friendship and account-ability are all about.

Boundary Line #4: Strive for excellence, not perfection

Excellence and perfectionism are two very different animals. Excellence means doing the best we can do within the time available. Perfectionism burns the candle at two ends and the middle as well, stretching us way beyond healthy limits. The hard side of our perfectionism isn't pretty. We lose our tolerance for others' humanity. We raise the hoops for everyone around us, from our young children and wife to our neighbors and co-workers. Our hearts harden because we have one goal: to beat everyone around us.

Maybe you work with a guy that has to have it all, at any cost. He is cutthroat, either overtly or subtly, going after his goal with a vengeance, leaving in his path a series of broken relationships. He may be number one in sales, in wins, in his territory, and in all the "right" numbers, but let's face it...*he's a loser.* The very goal that seemed so honorable in the beginning becomes hollow as his perfectionism and drivenness alienate all those around him, leaving his heart hardened and his castle purged.

How we need the perspective of Paul:

> But whatever was to my profit I now consider loss for the sake of Christ. What is more, I consider everything a loss compared to the surpassing greatness of knowing Christ Jesus my Lord, for whose sake I have lost all things. I consider them rubbish, that I may gain Christ and be found in him, not having a righteousness of my own that comes from the law, but that which is through faith in Christ —the righteousness that comes from God and is by faith. (Philippians 3:7-9)

The point? There's nothing wrong with competitiveness when we're pursuing excellence that honors the name of Christ. But when we cross the boundary line from excellence to perfectionism our "win" becomes our greatest loss. Christ can only be honored in our righteousness. And there is no righteousness in unchecked competition.

My good brother, let's glory in our competitive nature. Let's attack this thing called life with all our heart, soul, and strength, and reach for the highest and best. That's the way God wired us.

But in the heat and drive of our competition, let's commit together as men to stay within the boundaries He's laid down for us.

It's more fun that way.

And in the long run, it's the only strategy that wins.

Application Suggestions:

1. Think back over the last two or three months, and recall a situation in which your competitiveness was clearly in operation. Were any of the three "lethal elements"—pride, envy, and greed—a part of your competitiveness in that situation? On a sheet of paper, write down those three words, then rate that situation according to how much each one of those elements was present. Use a 1-to-10 scale: 1 = not a trace of this element was present, and 10 = this element was present in full force.

2. Now evaluate that situation again as you think about this chapter's conclusion: *"There's nothing wrong with competitiveness when we're pursuing excellence that honors the name of Christ."* Use a 1-to-10 scale to answer this question: How strong in that situation was my desire to honor Christ?

3. Keep the pattern of Philippians 4:6-7 in mind (prayer → God's peace → a guarded heart) as you write out a prayer that asks God to keep your competitiveness under the Holy Spirit's control. Express your desire to pursue an excellence that's motivated purely by the desire to glorify God.

To Think About & Discuss:

1. How can we men find a balance between passages such as Colossians 3:23 that urge us to be wholehearted and eager in whatever we do, and the many passages like Ephesians 4:2 and 1 Peter 3:8 that command us to be humble and gentle?

2. What did proud Naaman discover when he (finally, after much grousing) humbled himself to follow God's instructions to the letter (2 Kings 5:15)? What do we discover about God when we surrender our pride and walk the path of humble obedience?

3. The author quotes Proverbs 14:30 in his discussion about the "lethal element" of envy. In what way does envy rob us of peace? Based on this verse, describe what simple contentment can do for a man's life.

4. Restate Proverbs 4:25-27 in your own words. How does this passage speak to the matter of envy and greed?

5. The author cites "Examine your motives" as a major boundary line to restrain us from out-of-control competition. List three ways that adopting David's prayer in Psalm 139:23-24 could help you examine your motives.

....

CHAPTER THIRTEEN

CHRISTIANITY IS A TEAM SPORT

■

Two things are true for all of us.

First, we all need to get in shape and stay in shape.

Second, we don't have to do all of the training alone.

You can ride to the gym with a friend. You can work out next to a buddy. You can huff and puff and try to match your training with another man. You can be a spotter when a guy's on the bench pressing more weight than he's ever pressed before. You can grab a couple Cokes after you've hit the showers and have a few laughs together on the way home.

Training is tough. Training is sometimes monotonous, sometimes painful, and sometimes it takes all you have to stay with a program. But you don't have to sweat it out alone.

Life can be tough, too. But you don't have to work it through solo. Christianity is a *team* sport. Always has been, always will be. In fact, there are really only two things we can't do alone: one is to get married; the other is to be a Christian. In this chapter I want to talk to you about teaming up with other men in order to mature in your relationship with Jesus Christ. It takes more than one of us to grow as a Christian. God wired us to be relational beings.

Solomon penned that thought in Ecclesiastes, near the latter part of his life.

> Though one may be overpowered, two can defend themselves. A
> cord of three strands is not quickly broken. (Ecclesiastes 4:12)

We need each other. Men were meant to relate to each other. We were designed for companionship, not isolation. When we are alone, we run the risk of being overwhelmed by life. When we gather with at least one other, we are able to team up and defend ourselves. Solomon says a cord of three strands is not quickly broken. The strength of three men together is more capable of fighting off the sometimes overwhelming pain and challenges of everyday living on a broken planet.

Yet what do you see when you look around you? Many times we see men trying to do it alone. Men who claim they don't need anyone else. Men who isolate themselves from others, including their wives, kids, friends, parents, neighbors, and church family. Men who put up walls around themselves and suffer the natural result: loneliness.

That is not God's desire. He wants us to relate to each other. Christianity is indeed a team sport. Deep down, most of us long to be part of something bigger than we are. Unless our inner man has been completely torched and charred somewhere along the way, most of us would like to have a friend and be a friend. But since we don't know how to move out of cautious independence into friendship and mutual dependence, we pull away and pretend "it's no big deal" and "we don't really care anyway."

Through the pages of this book, we've gone through a survey of your castle, identifying weak spots on the perimeter as well as cracks on the inside walls. So let me ask you a question: *Where is your castle most vulnerable?* Is it the north wall? Does the moat need to be restocked with hungry alligators, ready to keep intruders at bay? Are the troops within the walls demoralized, needing fresh encouragement? Does the lady of the castle know you still have a vision for your marriage? For the future of your family?

What's your first assignment, friend? Do you need to redouble your defenses against a furious frontal attack? Have the invaders wormed through your protective walls through sneak attacks?

So what do we do about it? In this chapter, I want to challenge you on a key role of a CrossTrainer: to be more than just a casual buddy to other guys. In such a day and time as this, we need more than a golf partner. More than a guy who'll eat a hamburger with us and listen to us complain about the boss. More than a TV football chum who'll watch the game of the week with us.

We need men who will go to war with us. We need guys ready to strap on the armor and stand at our side as we do battle for our homes and families.

A CrossTrainer? He's a *warrior*. He's a man willing to stand in the line of fire with his brothers. He's a man willing to march alongside other men in a culture determined to pick off anyone who holds a righteous standard. He's a man willing to stand for something more important than his own selfish desires. He's the kind of guy who not only can quote a passage like 1 Corinthians 16:13-14, but also *lives* it.

> Be on your guard; stand firm in the faith; be men of courage; be strong. Do everything in love. (1 Corinthians 16:13-14)

Even though you and I know we need to team up with other guys, we fall into habitual patterns of isolation and self-reliance and hiding in shadows. And when we do, we are even more open to the attacks of the enemy. If we are to shield ourselves from Satan's poison-tipped arrows, one of the most basic strategies we can adhere to is to link up with other men. We need to face the challenges of living as Christ's men, leading our families, and confronting our culture *in partnership*.

One way to accomplish this goal is to learn to cross-train in our life roles: as believers in Jesus Christ, husbands, dads, friends, and citizens. Let me tell you about crosstraining, not as athletes on the track in a stadium, but as men on the track of life.

CrossTrainers

God wants you and I to win in our roles as husbands and dads. I believe He wants us to bring every resource to bear in order to attain that goal —and that means taking the risk to reach out for help and encouragement. That point finally got through my own thick skull when I was in crisis with my own family.

In the late seventies, I began attending a breakfast with a few guys from my church. About a dozen of us would meet weekly and hang out with each other to encourage, study, and pray for each other. That group fizzled after several months, but my need didn't. I finally got up the guts to ask three of the guys to continue meeting. I knew I needed help. So four of us continued on…and have ever since.

We would read Christian books to stretch us in our roles. We'd pray for each other. At times our sessions were heavy; at other times we'd do a lot of laughing. But one thing remained true: Our four hearts began to knit together.

Green Cards

One night after the 1992 Promise Keepers conference in Boulder, Colorado, our little band of accountability amigos stayed up late and asked each other a few tough questions, such as:

What are the three things you don't want anyone to know about you?

If you could identify three questions you'd prefer not to be asked on a regular basis, what would they be?

It took hours to go around the room asking each other, but by the end of that time we had written down twelve questions, three for each of us. More importantly, we made the commitment to each other that when we got back to Des Moines, we would ask each other these questions during our weekly accountability lunches.

After our return, one of the guys took our questions and printed them out on green cards, the size of a business card. All our questions are listed under each of our names. *And these questions are fair game for any of us, at any time.* On Tuesdays, during our accountability sessions, one of us will often whip our card from our wallet, lay it on the table, and start that sometimes uncomfortable dialogue. I've had a few unsettling lunches on Tuesdays where the Italian food didn't want to slide down very easily. But as unsettling as those questions have been on my digestive system, they've been producing growth in my spirit.

What exactly do the questions say? Quite frankly, it's none of your business. It's the business of our little group—our mutual business, by common consent. Because what each of us wrote down is specific to the areas where God is challenging us in our personal lives today.

Do you have a friend or group of friends in your life willing to ask you the tough questions? Men who will love you enough to not only celebrate your successes but also stand by you in your failures? Men who will stick closely by you during the bad times as well as good times, but will not fall into the trap of telling you only what you want to hear? Men who are willing to look you in the eye and ask you questions like these:

How's your thought life?

How are you handling the balance between work and home?

Have you been in the Word over the last few days?

What has God been teaching you recently?

How are you doing in handling God's provision of time, talent, and money?

Are you being responsible in protecting your eyes, hands, feet, and mind with women other than your wife?

Are you shooting straight in answering the above questions—or trying to blow smoke?

To the point? Yes indeed. Metal on metal. Iron sharpening iron.

After about ten years of meeting and laying our green cards out on the table, we knew God had a purpose for our friendships, a purpose that would prove to be the core of what has become CrossTrainers, a ministry to men both in Des Moines and beyond.

How did it go from four guys to hundreds? It all happened in the summer of '89.

A Landmark Summer

As I reviewed my upcoming counseling schedule for the month of June, I noticed the names of a couple of guys who I thought I'd wrapped up with. Yet they kept coming back, shelling out the bucks to meet with me in my office.

I was puzzled, so I gave each of them a call, saying basically the same thing to both men.

"What's going on? We've followed our plan. We've moved through our sessions together. You're doing a great job leading your family now. What's up?"

The two men had never spoken to one another, but each replied in essentially the same way: "Gary, you're the only man I know well enough to be honest with. I feel isolated—like I'm the only guy out there struggling with stuff. I just need to talk things through, you know? So I thought I'd continue in counseling to get the feedback I know I need if I'm going to keep making progress with my family."

These two guys got my attention. You know why? Because they were both just like me. Yet I remember telling both of these guys that this was pretty expensive friendship, so why not just grab lunch together from time to time? It sounded like a good idea, but both of these guys knew my schedule was stretched already, and neither one of them wanted to impose.

The next Tuesday in my own small group, I told my three accountability partners about my experience. Then I threw an idea on the table that ended up changing all of our lives.

"It's your call," I told my friends, "but my idea is to invite these two guys— and maybe eight or nine other guys who've been trying to break into our foursome for the last several years—to a weekly study on men and their roles. What do you think?"

I remember thinking, *Hey, this would be a great way to get some of these guys together to encourage each other, allow me to continue to hang out with some of the guys needing a little extra boost, and lighten up my own counseling schedule a little.* I even offered my conference room and volunteered Barbara to make some of her world-class muffins. What a deal. No one passed it up.

Twelve of us met for twelve weeks on Wednesday mornings, read Pat Morley's book *The Man in the Mirror,* drank some coffee, and put away some of the best muffins west of the Mississippi. On the eleventh session I was out making some more coffee and came back to the conference room with an announcement.

"Well guys, next week is our last week. It's been great, but now it's time to wrap up."

I received a curious response.

"Rosberg, while you were out of the room we voted unanimously to keep going. We don't care if you come or not, but we do want your conference room —and more importantly, we want Barb to keep making the muffins!"

Two weeks later we had almost 20 guys and launched into a new book study. A few months later it was 35 guys, then 60, then 100—driving in from a 75-mile radius of Des Moines. Now more than 450 men from 70 churches and 22 denominations call themselves CrossTrainers. Hundreds of us converge on a local restaurant every Wednesday morning for some teaching, mutual encouragement, and accountability. The group has grown out of its morning space, so we launched a second lunch-hour group in the downtown financial district of the city. The first week's attendance was 85. (I was hoping for 15!)

Truthfully, I keep waiting for this phenomenon called CrossTrainers to slow down a little, so that we can catch our collective breath. But it shows no sign of slowing down. Now some of you are saying, "Hey, what *else* is there to do in Des Moines at 6:45 in the morning?" But guys keep coming. Men who know Christ and men who don't. Men who've lost their marriages, men who are on the brink of it, men who have rock-solid marriages, and men who are still looking for Miss Right.

We had a sixteen-year-old who asked his dad after a first visit: "Dad, I want to *be* a CrossTrainer and come every week."

Just this past week, a man asked if "other religions" are welcome. He's a Hindu, and let me tell you…we'll make him welcome.

Why is CrossTrainers impacting so many men? Because (once again for emphasis) we need each other! No, it isn't always easy to admit, but it's true. Think about it. When you were kids, what did you do? After your chores were done (or sometimes before they were done), you went outside and played. Nintendos and remote controls weren't in our world yet, just playing ball, building tree houses, riding bikes, and hanging out with our buddies. It was great. Oh sure, sometimes you'd fight with them, but they were your pals, and they were in your life day in and day out.

But then something happened in adolescence (besides zits and a little extra hair): We discovered girls. One by one a lot of the guys began to drop off and started hanging around the fairer sex. It was part of life and inevitable, but the loss of our buddies left a hole in us—a need for other guys. After high school we headed off for the service, work, or college and got some new friends. But by the time we settled down and got married, a lot of us tended to lose our male friends. Oh, we promised we wouldn't lose touch—and some of us have retained contact with a few of the guys—but most of us go our separate ways. Other men tend not to play a big role in our lives. We get used to trying to juggle life alone…and that's when we start losing our grip and dropping some pretty important items.

We may play softball, go hunting, or watch a game together, but it becomes easier and easier to lose meaningful contact with other men. Our schedules are *full enough* just trying to get careers going, pay our bills, and spend time with our wives and kids. So the guys take the back seat…but if you look in the rear view mirror, a lot of those back seats are empty. Relationships that go unattended begin to fade fast, don't they?

We need other men in our lives. Men to hang out with, to grow in Christ with. We need friends who know us well enough to call us to account for some things when they see our life veering off the path. We need other guys in our lives to pray for us, to mentor us, and at times just to listen to us.

That's why CrossTrainers is taking off. Just as Jabez cried out to God, "Oh that you would bless me and enlarge my territory!" (1 Chronicles 4:10), we've seen God roll back our borders. We now have chapters in ten other cities from California to the Carolinas.

There's a great big hunger in men's hearts across America. No doubt it's been there for years. And now men are finally finding their way to the table.

How Does It Work?

What we do at CrossTrainers isn't that fancy or sophisticated. Each Wednesday morning cars pour into a parking lot before the sun comes up. We get together and have coffee and donuts, I teach something about the roles of men and we break into "A Teams" (accountability groups) to dig a little deeper.

And men come.

Some come because they're curious, some to grab some caffeine and cholesterol, others to grab a lifeline to pull them through a lake of deep pain in their lives. We have married guys, divorced guys, and guys enduring marital separation. We have gray-maned widowers as well as young men struggling with their sexuality and needing models of real men. We have dads, granddads, and wannabe dads. We have unemployed men, executives, blue-collar men, enough doctors to start a hospital, and the Governor of Iowa. We have men who have walked with Jesus Christ for many years, men who haven't darkened a church door in a quarter century, and men who are taking their first wobbly baby steps of faith.

Bottom line, we have men who want and thirst for help to be what God wants them to be. Real men. Leaders in the home. Sons of the Great King.

The CrossTrainer dynamic can happen with three hundred or with three or four men sitting around a table in the local waffle shop. But don't be impressed with the size of the group. Be impressed with the need. That's why we do CrossTrainers. We *need* it. We need the information, the support, and the challenge.

If you want to know more about CrossTrainers and how to start one in your own local pancake house, church, or living room, my address is in the front of the book. Write me. There are a team of guys in the middle of Iowa who'd love to help launch you.

An Urgent Warning

One morning during the early weeks of CrossTrainers, I'd just wrapped up the meeting with a closing prayer when I felt an urgency to say something else. Something more. A warning.

I don't get those kinds of feelings often, so I thought I'd better speak up.

"Hey guys," I said, "remember Sergeant Esterhaus on Hill Street Blues? You know, the cop who would always say, 'Let's be careful out there'? That's a good word, but I have a different message. *Guard your hearts, men.*"

It was pretty quiet in the room after that. I guess I'd spoken it with a surge of emotion. Guys looked at each other and I found myself wondering, *Now where in the world did that come from?*

You and I both know where it came from. It came from the Lord pricking my heart with the message of Proverbs 4:23. I'd never thought much about that verse—until it came pouring out of my heart that day over a table littered with napkins and empty coffee cups. I looked around the room at that little group of guys committed to crossing the finish line together and the words bubbled up unbidden.

Guard your hearts, men.

With that, they all left the room. As I was cleaning up the coffee cups and munching on a last muffin, I thought, *God, that is really the message You desire to convey, isn't it? Guard your heart. When you get right down to it, nothing matters more than the condition of our hearts. The heart truly is the wellspring of our lives. And out of it will come our life stories.*

Out of your heart will come your life story, my friend. We can encourage each other as men in the developing and refining of our stories, but ultimately, each of us must stand before God with the open pages of our own life. And every word will be read.

At the end of the next week's meeting, I closed with the same admonition. *Guard your hearts, men.*

And that's the way every CrossTrainers meeting has closed since 1989.

Part of the reason we keep saying that is because of the feedback we get from some of the men.

"Rosberg, sometimes I'm sitting in my hotel room on the road, flipping through the channels. When the temptation arises to sample some of the garbage, I think of the guys at CT, and I think of the words *guard your heart*. It gives me just the check I need to flip the tube off and keep it off."

"Several times I've come up against real ethical dilemmas in my job. I can think of two or three big crossroads when I could have gone one way or another. Then I think about what it would be like to have my 'A Team' in the room. And I think about you telling me to guard my heart. I'll be honest, Gary, it's pulled me back from the edge more than once."

"Last night I was so fed up at home. I found my temper getting ready to blow. Suddenly I thought about being with the guys on Wednesday and telling them about it. It was wild, Gary. It really put a check on my heart. I do want to guard my heart — I just sometimes forget in the heat of the moment."

Why should we guard our heart? First, because our main purpose in this life is to bring glory to Jesus Christ. When you face Jesus Christ, you want Him to look at you and say, "Well done, My good and faithful servant." Second, you want to prepare your family for life without you. You want their lives to please God, to carry your legacy into the next generation.

That's it. It isn't that complicated to figure out God's plan for us: to please and bring glory to Him and to prepare ourselves and our families for eternal life with Him. Guard your heart, for it is the wellspring of life. Our life stories will flow out of it. We need to guard it *fiercely*.

A man, a real man, crosstrains in five areas of life: with Christ, with his wife, with his kids, with his friends, with his community. A CrossTrainer guards his heart. A CrossTrainer is on the alert for frontal attacks as well as sneak attacks. A CrossTrainer not only starts the race, but finishes it well.

And perhaps most strategically, a CrossTrainer knows he can't do it alone. He knows he'll make it only in the company of some faithful buddies who are committed to him and to each other. He knows a cord of three strands is not easily broken.

Guarding your heart. It's a team sport... So find that team.

Application Suggestions:

1. Write down (a) three things that you don't want anyone to know about you, and (b) three personal questions that you'd prefer not to be asked on a regular basis.

2. Are you a part of a group of men—two or more—who are committed to each other in the way described in this chapter? If not, what immediate step can you take to find someone to buddy up with?

3. Keep the pattern of Philippians 4:6-7 in mind (prayer → God's peace → a guarded heart) as you write out a prayer that asks God to give you the encouragement and support from other men that you need. Ask Him to faithfully provide these brothers for the rest of your life on earth.

To Think About & Discuss:

1. Ecclesiastes 4:9-12 makes the point that "two are better than one." Now go back and read the previous two verses, 7 and 8. In your own words, describe the experience of one man determined to fly solo.

2. How might Solomon's sad life experience have been different if he had *lived* his own counsel in Ecclesiastes 4:10?

3. What wisdom and counsel does Hebrews 10:4-5 contribute to the author's theme that "Christianity is a team sport"?

4. Now turn back a few pages in your Bible to Hebrews 3:12-14. According to this passage, what vital role does mutual encouragement play in the life of a believer? What is the significance of the word "daily" in verse 13?

CHAPTER FOURTEEN

THREE ROCKS

∎

I collect rocks. Not necessarily physically, but in my memory bank. In fact, I have three in particular that have special meaning for me:

- One failed to contain a Nazarene carpenter.
- One witnessed a furious spiritual battle.
- The last provides a castle's foundation.

They're three very different kind of rocks. The first you can find in the Bible; the second sits in my wife's jewelry box; the third undergirds the homes of wise men all over the world. May I show you my rock collection? Each of these rocks represents an aspect of our faith in God.

The Rock That Couldn't Hold the Savior

Rocks are mentioned throughout Scripture. But one rock stands out perhaps more than any other. It is the rock that was rolled in front of a tomb to hold in the lifeless body of God's Son, a body that was resurrected to sit at the right hand of the Father. The Roman governor Pilate thought a huge rock, an official seal, and a contingent of tough Roman guards would keep Jesus from fulfilling His word about rising from the grave. But neither the rock, the official seal, the Roman guard, the religious officials, nor the times could hold Him in.

Why? Because God had another plan. Christ's resurrection was central to God's purpose for humankind. Without it we would have no hope of eternal life. Praise God, the rock was moved, despite the best efforts of Pilate and the Roman guard.

Did it take an army to overwhelm the guard? No—all it took was a single angel. After the angel had moved aside the stone, Jesus appeared to Mary Magdalene and the other Mary and later to the disciples. He had risen! The single most important event in the history of man.

Some today no doubt wonder—couldn't the guard have slept while the disciples moved the stone and removed their Lord's still, lifeless body? Not likely. These soldiers were the crackerjack members of the guard. They didn't sleep on duty—the penalty for grabbing forty winks was death. There is one and only one explanation for why the rock moved: The rock moved because God knew that mere men (like me) would sit back and try to disprove the truth. But it also moved because men (like me), when faced with the truth, might accept it and allow it to change our lives.

Make no mistake. The rock moved, just as Scripture says. Jesus' resurrection is the key to the Christian life.

My Rock

There is a second rock that has tremendous meaning for my life. Many years ago I held onto it for dear life in the midst of a ferocious battle over my very soul. Let me take you back with me to the most important night of my life.

I was hanging out over at Barbara's parents' house one evening. We had been dating for five or six months as college students, and we went over to her folks' house for a chicken and dumpling dinner. As the evening progressed, something came over me. Such a compulsion has only happened to me a few times since. I can only describe it as an indescribable need to be alone. Actually, not all alone, but to be invited into God's presence. His outstretched hand beckoned me. I answered and my life story was altered for eternity.

But perhaps I should back up. Over the several months preceding that evening, Barbara and some guys at Drake (my college) were explaining to me something I had never heard: that we could have a personal relationship with

Jesus Christ. That sounded weird to me. I just couldn't quite get it. It seemed so simple, yet so complex.

I grew up in a family that respected God and went to church, but no one ever explained to me the possibility of enjoying a *personal* relationship with Christ. Within a couple weeks of meeting Barb, who had just become a Christian, I also met some guys from a group called Campus Crusade for Christ. They spoke at my fraternity house and for the first time in my life I heard that Christ died for *me*. It sounded so good. But my pride got in the way. I took a skeptic's approach and set out to disprove the truth of the resurrection of Christ.

I studied, tore into the Scriptures, met with Christians, and tried a local church where the gospel was taught. I asked question after question of anyone who would listen. A man named Gordon Mooney from Campus Crusade led the pack in trying to help me sort out this new information that was flooding my mind. I listened to Barbara discuss her new-found life and was torn apart. On one hand, I wanted nothing more than to accept that Jesus Christ died for me and my sins. On the other hand, my pride was so strong that I found myself running from the truth, fearing the changes God would make in my life. Yet the more I allowed God's truth to sink in, the more I realized He was going to change everything about my life. In my heart I knew I needed to yield to Him.

So by the time I got to that summer night in 1973—after snarfing down some chicken and dumplings—I found myself compelled to be alone. All I knew was that I needed to get away.

I had no idea I was on my way to a war.

I stood up to excuse myself, which confused Barb. She thought we were going to a movie or something. "Barb," I said, "I just need to be alone for a while. I am going to take a walk." Then I headed out the door. I found myself several minutes later in a soon-to-be-poured parking lot for a neighborhood grocery store. As I approached, I came upon a pile of rocks destined to be used under the concrete. The next thing I knew, I was sitting on top of the rocks.

Over the next hour or so a war began between God and myself over who would lay claim to the real estate of my very soul. I sat on top of that pile of rocks, picked up a stone, and held on to it with all of my heart. I began to pray. "God, I don't know why You would want a man like me. I have disappointed You, my parents, Barb, and myself. I blow it every time I turn around—but the more I learn about You, the more I know that it is You I need in my heart. It seems so simple to ask, but I just can't seem to do it."

But even as I found myself crying out to Him, I felt another power pulling me away.

Just as I would begin to feel calmed in my ragged prayers, I would sense turbulence rising up against the calm. It was as if the enemy was saying, *Why would God want you, Gary? You have screwed up relationships, decisions, you name it. You aren't worth it! God wants only the best, and you are nothing but a loser. You may look okay on the outside, but inside, I know you! You are selfish and prideful. You want things your way, not God's way. He isn't for you. And you aren't for Him.*

I know this may sound like a scene from some cheap cable TV show, but it isn't. It happened. As the battle raged, I held onto that rock. I told both God and Satan that if I were to accept God as my Lord that night, I would hang on to that rock for as long as He would allow me to. But if I rejected Him, I would throw that rock as hard and far as I could, and never seek Him again.

The war went on a long time. The very rocks seemed to scream out. God on one side, Satan on the other. "Seek and you will find" was countered by, "Who would care whether *you* found him?" "I died for you, son. Come to Me and I will give you rest for your soul," received the return volley: "Who needs rest? Live life any way you want. Do your own thing!" A gracious inner voice said, "I am the everlasting, the Alpha and the Omega." A seductive tongue replied, "I will meet your every pleasure—women, greed, indulgences. Come my way! Forget the narrow road! My road is open territory to do what you want. Who would want to walk a narrow road?"

It was that last salvo that got me. "God is the Alpha and the Omega." I knew that He was the beginning and the end, that He created the world, the earth, and the heavens, and that He will reign forever. I knew at that moment where my heart had to be.

Suddenly, it was clear. My heart had to be turned over to the only One who sticks by you every time. The only One who will never come up short. The only One who loves you and knows your anxious thoughts, your mistakes, your major league foulups... and still sticks by you. My heart needed to be with the One who gave His only Son so that I could have life. My heart needed to be opened to let Him in, to experience life, both life on this earth and with Him eternally.

As I sat on that rock pile hanging onto that stone, I cried out to God.

"God, I don't know why You would want me. I am selfish and prideful. I do my own thing and go my own way. But the more I learn about You, the more I realize that You do have a plan for me. You've brought people into my life, both Barb and these guys at school who proclaim You. I want to know You like they do. I know I have sinned. And God, I ask You to forgive me for those sins. I ask You to come into my heart, right now, right on this rock pile. God, I want You to be more than just my Savior. I want You to be my Lord."

And He did. Right there.

As I finished that prayer, it was as if the weight of that entire rock pile was lifted from my shoulders. I was free, the chains were broken, the war was over. I knew who won—God did. He was willing to go to war for me! I looked down at my clenched fist, sweat and tears pouring down my face, and I opened my hand. There I saw the rock I had gripped so tightly during my war. I knew I needed to leave that rock pile, but there was something within me that wanted to stay there forever. A parking lot had become a sanctuary!

Immediately I found a phone booth in a drugstore where Barbara had bought candy as a young girl. I called that young, courageous woman who had stood so firm for Christ (and who, twenty-four months later, would walk down the aisle with me to become my one and only.)

"Barb, I need you to meet me down the street," I said. "I'm at your drugstore. I need to talk to you. No questions, please. Just meet me halfway."

As we approached each other under the street light, from about thirty feet away she looked at me and called out, "You just accepted Jesus Christ!" Her face was beaming like I had never seen before. I remember saying, "Is that how this thing works? When you accept Christ, you just know those things?"

We laugh about my question now. But sometimes you *do* know things. Every once in a while God gives us a glimpse through the window of another's soul, and we see the hope as well as the hurt. My lady had seen the hope!

I still have that rock. I keep it in Barbara's jewelry box. Today it is sitting on the table next to me as I write. For over twenty years God has allowed me to keep it—not as an idol, just as a memorial. I may lose it today. If so, no big deal, because what it reflects is in my heart, stored for eternity. It reminds me of the night when my life story was altered forever, a night when my independence gave way to my dependence, a night when God went to war against Satan to show me once again He loves me so much that He gave up His own Son to die on my behalf. That rock silently reminds me that the most selfless act of all of history was performed to provide life for a selfish guy like me.

A Rock that Will Support a Castle

One more rock before I close this chapter. It is the rock we build our castle upon. Listen…

> Therefore, everyone who hears these words of mine and puts them into practice is like a wise man who built his house on the rock. The rain came down, the streams rose and the winds blew and beat against that house; yet it did not fall, because it had its foundations on the rock. But everyone who hears these words of mine and does not put them into practice is like a foolish man who built his house on sand. The rain came down, the streams rose, and the winds blew and beat against that house, and it fell with a great crash. (Matthew 7:24-27)

That castle or house is our faith. When our faith is built upon the rock of Almighty God, we can withstand anything life might throw against us. The foundation of my faith and yours is a relationship with the rock, Jesus Christ. To build upon the rock means to be obedient, to be sure, to have a solid foundation. Sandy foundations didn't secure castles in Europe, nor will they secure our faith in stormy weather. A castle built on sand may look good on a clear day when the sun shines in its strength, but when the storm clouds begin to brew, such a castle is in deep trouble.

A lot of us don't think about our foundation until the storm hits. Then we regret our sloppy workmanship. We must build our castles in such a way that whether we're in the storms of life—sick kids, overwhelming bills, marital pain, stress—or in a clear-sailing day and everything is going great, we know that the foundation beneath us will stand there immovable. Like a rock.

What kind of foundation supports your castle?

A Crossroads

Perhaps right now you have come to a crossroads.

On one hand, you can choose to go your own way. On the other hand, you can choose God's way. And I'm not just talking about coming into a right relationship with God through faith in Jesus Christ. A lot of men have made "decisions" for Christ (as a kind of fire insurance) but have firmly decided to set their own course. I can't imagine a more miserable trip.

A man determined to choose God's way above all else may indeed find a road sometimes full of potholes, but he'll also know that God has promised on oath that He will never leave him nor forsake him. God will bring such a man into His kingdom and lavish upon him eternal life.

Does that sound like a good deal? It is! All you have to do is ask. You don't need to climb a rock pile. You don't need to disprove or prove anything; that's already been done.

You just need to ask.

If you want to do that right now, let me with deepest respect suggest a prayer that can help you walk through it:

> God, I don't know why You would want me. I have fallen way short and have sinned against You. I confess those sins and am sorry. And God, I ask You right now to come into my life. I receive You into my heart as my Lord and Savior and ask You to forgive me of my sins. Lord, help me to be the kind of man You want me to be.

That's it. Simple? Yes. Easy? Only if you can let go of your pride. My prayer for you is that you will know the Father. He is the rock.

By the way, let me know if you pray that prayer.

The Rock of Our Faith

Real men, men who hunger and thirst after Jesus Christ, know that a living, vital relationship with God is their number one purpose in life. Men who want to lead their families effectively realize that if this relationship isn't on the top of the heap, then nothing else will much matter. They know that when they rely on anything else, it will come up short. But He never will.

My challenge to you is to realize that serving God is the most important purpose we have in life. If you tried to guard your heart in all other areas except this one, you would be certain to fail in all of them. Your relationship to God is the linchpin of all else.

Guard your heart—especially in your walk with God. Nothing is more important. Nothing is more pressing. Nothing!

Yet nothing promises such extravagant rewards.

What a God we serve!

Application Suggestions:

1. Are you determined to choose God's way above all else? Decide now to set aside at least one half-hour sometime in the next three days to get alone with God, and to talk with Him openly about your current level of commitment to Him, and about what you have learned while reading this book.

2. Look back through this book at the chapter titles, and at the application suggestions following each chapter. Make a list of (a) the most important things you have learned from this book, and (b) the most important things you need to do now for the sake of your relationship with God, with your wife, and with your children.

To Think About & Discuss:

1. Read Matthew 27:59-66. What did the stone, seal, and guard before Jesus' tomb represent to the religious and governmental authorities? What then, was God's message to these same officials when the stone was tossed aside, the seal was broken, and the guard disabled? What is the message to the whole world? What is the message to *you?*

2. Realizing that God is the sovereign "Alpha and Omega" finally led Gary to surrender his life to the Lordship of Jesus Christ. What verse, idea, word picture, or compelling need finally brought *you* "over the top" into a relationship with Him? How might you explain that crucial, pivotal thought in a brief two-to-three-minute testimony that could help nudge other struggling seekers into receiving God's gift of salvation?

3. Look up the following passages and discuss how they specifically apply to a dad who wants to lead in his family and bring stability to his home. Psalm 18:2, 27:5, 31:3, 40:2, 61:2, and 144:1.

GUARDING YOUR LIFE STORY

■

Guard your heart...
for out of it will flow your life story.

I began this book with a puzzling life story. Remember Barney O'Malley? He was a man whose life ended in a curious tangle of questions, mysteries, and frayed loose ends.

A man who never married.

A man who fathered a child, but remained alone.

A man who traveled from city to city, spinning his yarns.

A man who stacked up worthless items like a pack rat, but left nothing of value behind.

A man who continually misled others, not because he was a bad man, but because he wanted so much to impress people and somehow make his mark.

A man who tried to navigate the shoals and channels of life with neither map nor chart, but never found his way.

That was Barney's life story. A sad and empty one. But just last night, I encountered a life story of a very different sort.

It began at a backyard graduation party, a soft spring twilight alive with the music of cicadas and bird songs, the air fragrant with a sizzling barbecue. I'd never met Bill and Peg Keul until Barbara and I had the privilege of sitting next to them at a picnic table. Barbara was already seated when I wandered over with my loaded plate to join her. Smiling a greeting at the other folks at the table, I sat down and prepared to dive in. Just as I was about to take a bite of food, Barbara said, "Gary, Bill and Peg are the parents of Jeff—the young Wheaton student who was killed a few months ago."

I put my fork down again. I'd heard about the accident through some friends at church.

It was Jeff's first hockey game for Wheaton College in suburban Chicago. At 3:40 a.m., on January 29, 1994, as the team returned from a game with Bradley University, the van Jeff was riding in with five teammates hit a disabled truck parked along the road. The other five young men were all hospitalized. Jeff was the only one to lose his life.

It was a tragedy felt not only by the family, but by the entire Wheaton College community. The loss of a gifted young man. A young man destined to make a difference.

And he has.

A Mom and a Dad Celebrate a Life Story

As the twilight deepened above our backyard party, Bill and Peg reflected on Jeff's life through tears and laughter. His memory was a strong presence at our little table. Jeff's mom smiled and dabbed at her eyes, telling of how Jeff would call home from college during the day to chat with her, then call back that same evening and repeat the same stories to his dad. They talked about Jeff's recent call into full time ministry. About his commitment to go to Haiti on a missions trip. About his newly awakened desire to preach God's Word.

While Bill and Peg had opened their home to thirty-six adoptive and foster children through the years, Jeff had been their only biological son. They talked about the impact of his life on all the little ones who filled their home.

Bill recalled how three-year-old Kristopher had recently been helping him dump the grass clippings. When Bill complimented the little guy on his work, Kristopher replied, "Jesus and Jeff taught me how to do this, Dad."

"What do you think Jesus and Jeff are doing right now?" Bill asked him.

"Oh," he replied, "they're probably praying and singing. And getting ready for bed."

Guests came and left as Barb and I walked with the Keuls through their pride and pain. As I listened, questions rang in my head, *Why, God? Why take Your finest home so soon—so early in life? Why remove a life so rich with promise, so brimming with potential?*

I couldn't help wondering how I would handle this kind of loss, and found myself stealing over-the-shoulder glances at Sarah, my sixteen-year-old. She was happily planning an evening out with her best friend, Shelley. There would be a swimming party and a trip to McDonalds afterward. Through her laughter, Bill's words kept swirling in my head, "You know, Gary, you always worry about your kids when they head off in cars, but you never really think anything could happen to *your* kids. It's always someone else's children."

I thought of Missy, my little one who isn't so little anymore. She's turning thirteen in three days, and looking forward to a Memorial Day weekend at a friend's lake cottage. I found myself shooting up a telegraph prayer. *Dear Father, keep her in Your care.*

Jeff Keul lived such a brief life with his family. But brief as it was, it was rich and filled with purpose.

He did not leave a puzzling life story behind.

He did not leave a tangled web of empty boasts, half-truths, and deceptions.

He did not leave a set of winding, wandering, aimless footprints.

He did not leave a jumbled, muddled, chaotic legacy to sift through after his departure.

No one had to puzzle over Jeff's life and wonder who he was and what he was all about. His life story, abbreviated by an untimely death, stands clear and open for all to read. He was sold out to Jesus Christ. He loved his Lord, loved his family, and loved his friends. All who were touched by his life—his parents, his friends, his college, his church, and his thirty-six "brothers and sisters"—feel more wide awake to eternal realities and hungrier for heaven…because of Jeff.

Some 1,200 people came to visit Jeff's family before the funeral, then 750 crammed into the little Baptist church in Winterset, Iowa, for the service. Later, another 2,300 attended a memorial service at Wheaton.

Jeff, you see, finished the race well. In a way he probably never could have imagined, Jeff's life echoed the great apostle's parting words to the church at Ephesus:

> I consider my life worth nothing to me, if only I may finish the race and complete the task the Lord Jesus has given me—the task of testifying to the gospel of God's grace. (Acts 20:24)

Jeff Keul's race is over now, and he finished strong. But you and I are still in the race, aren't we? We're still running. We're still stretching toward the tape. The finish line is still up ahead. For some of us, it's many years down the road. For others it may be just around the next bend. The fact is, none of us know when we'll cross that line.

Perhaps like me, you find yourself wondering at times.

How will I finish the race? How will my life story read? What will be the legacy I leave behind? Will my friends and family review my life and find me faithful?

That's what struck me so as I reflected on the life stories of Barney O'Malley, and then Jeff Keul. Barney's story is over, and frankly, he left a mess. His legacy of lies, wandering, and multilayered enigmas touched no one. His name is already fading from this earth, like a passing shadow on the sidewalk. In the end, his life was as futile and pointless as a studio apartment stuffed with used toasters.

Jeff's earthly story is over, too. But young as he was, he left a mighty legacy. His example and his passing have marked his friends, family, and classmates for life…for eternity. Through this book, his life even reaches up through print and paper to touch you as well.

Just for a moment, let's go back to Paul's emotional farewell on the sandy shore of the blue Aegean Sea. He was saying goodbye to those he held dear. He knew he would not see them again, at least not in this life. But make no mistake about it. He knew that if they had placed their faith in Jesus Christ, he would see them again in the Lord's presence.

> Now I know that none of you among whom I have gone about preaching the kingdom will ever see me again. Therefore, I declare to you today that I am innocent of the blood of all men. For I have not hesitated to proclaim to you the whole will of God. Keep watch over yourselves and all the flock of which the Holy Spirit has made you overseers. Be shepherds of the church of God, which he bought with his own blood. I know that after I leave, savage wolves will come in among you and will not spare the flock. Even from your own number men will arise and distort the truth in order to draw away disciples after them. So be on your guard!
> (Acts 20:25-31)

Be On Your Guard

Paul challenges all of us as men to finish the race and to be on our guard. Why does he do that? Because he knows that even if we've built a positive legacy to this point, there are wolves waiting at the door, ready to tear it from our grip and steal it away. He knows that we can lose our testimony, our counsel, and our influence as a role model *in a single unguarded moment.* What a frightening thought! One carelessly spilled bottle of black ink can seep through the pages of your entire life story. One drop of toxic selfishness can taint and poison the wellspring of your life. One moment of leaving the castle door unguarded can invite a cruel invasion.

That is Paul's sobering message to us. It's also Solomon's message. Remember this little entry from his journal, recorded in the book of Proverbs?

> I walked by the field of a certain lazy fellow and saw that it was overgrown with thorns, and covered with weeds; and its walls were broken down. Then, as I looked, I learned this lesson:
> "A little extra sleep,
> a little more slumber,
> a little folding of the hands to rest"
> means that poverty will break in upon you suddenly like a robber, and violently like a bandit. (Proverbs 24:30-34, TLB)

Don't let anyone steal your legacy. Don't let anyone rob a lifetime of influence on your wife, your children, your friends, and your neighbors. Don't let moral poverty sneak up on you like a slinking wolf and rip away your witness for Jesus Christ. Guard your heart, man! Guard it with every ounce of energy you possess. Guard it in the limitless, fathomless, bottomless power of God's indwelling Spirit.

But don't stand guard alone.

You need some fellow warriors at your side. You need some buddies to watch your path. You need a few good men to pray for you, encourage you, teach you, walk with you, and remind you of what you already know. And by the way, there are some guys out there who need the same thing from you! A listening ear. A wise word. An arm around the shoulder. A brotherly nudge in the right direction.

That's the way it works. God equips each of us, and we equip each other. God strengthens each of us, and we strengthen each other. God warns each of us, and we warn each other. God encourages each of us, and we encourage each other.

Finish well, my brother. Be strong. Be ready for the obstacles to increase, the enemies to multiply at your front gate, and the saboteurs to become slicker and more proficient at the attack. Put on the armor, the full armor of God.

Somehow, it seems appropriate to end this journey together with a prayer. I want to join you in that prayer. If I was with you in person or speaking to you in a conference setting, I would challenge you to stand. And friend, I would stand with you. So let's do that. Let's stand together in honor of our Father, right now. Whether you're in bed, in your easy chair, on a bus, or in your office, move into a standing position with me now as we commit the rest of our life stories to Him.

Dear Father,

You know so well who I am. Just a man. Just a package of dust, who lives a few years on this planet and then moves on. You know all about me, Father. My desires. My longings. My insecurities and fears. You also know, Lord, that I'm a man with dreams. I dream of a better life for me, my wife, my kids, and this hurting, bleeding, mixed-up nation you've placed me in.

God, please empower me with Your own Holy Spirit to finish the race well. I commit my life to You. I commit myself to finishing the race with the wife You've given me at my side.

Better than anyone else, Lord, You know I can't do it alone. I need You. I need the strength of brothers who love You.

Forgive me for my sins, in Jesus' name. Make me the kind of man that You want me to be. A leader of my family. A man willing to take Your message to a needy world.

And God, I will give You all the glory.

Thanks for the privilege of calling You Daddy.

Amen.

As soon as I step into heaven, I look forward to embracing an eternally young man named Jeff. And I look forward to a heavenly high-five with you, my brother.

See you at the finish line.

And whatever you do…above all else, guard your heart.

ONE MORE STEP

■

I am honored that you have stayed with me throughout this book. Like any author, I hope my words have instructed, encouraged, and stretched you. And I hope *Guard Your Heart* will do one more thing: challenge you to be accountable.

We've talked about becoming accountable to other men. Now I want to take it one more step—to give you a ritual that allows you to also increase your accountability to your wife.

In doing this, I've called on my best friend, Barbara.

As I envisioned the impact of this book, I knew its message could be strengthened by bringing you a message from Barb. As we talked about that idea, she gave me an even better one: allowing her to write to your wife, offering her encouragement and insight with which your lady can help you, her man, to guard your heart and finish the race well.

Obviously as you've read *Guard Your Heart* you've noticed that the last section of the book is sealed. The reason? The information within the sealed section is for your wife's eyes and heart, just as the body of the book is for yours. That doesn't mean you can't each read one another's pages here, but it does mean that Barbara and I have teamed up specifically to encourage you both as husband and wife.

So here is your charge, friend:

Take this book to your wife. Tell her of your desire to have her by your side.

Tell her how you need her in your life to complete you as a man. Share with her some insight that the book has given you.

Then instruct her to break the seal.

Behind the seal is the "key" to your heart, a woman's insight into her role of helping you guard your heart and fulfill God's desire for you as a man.

Take the risk, man. Go for it! And get ready for God to take your marriage to a higher level.

Helping Your Husband Guard His Heart

by Barbara Rosberg

■

To you, who like so many women,
have prayed for a book to challenge and equip
your husband—your knight in shining armor—
to guard his heart from the unending temptations
and pressures hurled at him continuously
by our contaminated world.

Gaze with me at this picture: In your hand is a key. Your knight has entrusted you, his elite lady, with this key. It is a master key to something yet undiscovered in his inner self.

Before you stands a castle. In fact, it's your knight's castle, well-guarded, with strong battlements in place. A locked gate in the fortress beckons you. You approach the gate, position the key, turn it in the lock, and enter. The gate closes securely behind you.

Within the fortified walls of his castle you cross a grassy courtyard which lures you beyond to a dark, secret passageway. You follow this narrow corridor, which you sense has never before been infiltrated by woman or the light of day.

You come to the corridor's end, and there you stand, startled. Your eyes behold a room filled with jeweled treasure, brilliant and bountiful, treasure that has lain guarded and untouched for a lifetime, hedged and hidden deep in the center of your knight's castle.

This is why he has guarded his castle, dearest lady. Here lies the rarest, most choice and precious of riches: *the vast treasure of his heart.* This wealth represents the core of his whole person, the hub of all his activity. It encompasses his feelings, his will, and even his intellect. It's the totality of his inner self.

You look again at the key in your hand. Only *you* hold the key to this heart.

And now you understand: You can help your husband take a stand with men of knighthood and nobility. You can help him stand shoulder-to-shoulder with valiant brothers, allied together in royal service to the King of kings. In a unique way, you can help him guard his heart for achieving the genuine manhood which is his special calling from God.

Perhaps this word picture has given you an inside look into your husband's heart. My friend, you hold the keys to open the door of his heart.

Gary and I have listened to couples all across the country tell us about their marriages and their needs. Now I would like to take these few pages to give you seven keys to understanding your husband. These keys are yours to help him guard his heart, and to finish the race as a couple committed to Jesus Christ.

But before we discuss these seven keys, we as wives need to realize that we have the power to either help or hurt our husbands. Make no mistake—we have significant influence on our men.

Help Him, or Hurt Him

You may be thinking, *Hey, you don't know my husband.* And you're right, I don't. But I don't need to. No doubt your husband has made mistakes in his past. All men, like all women, are fallible. Wrong choices can chisel away at the character of any of us, and diminished character can lead to the erosion of relationships. Thoughtless error can take down those who are closest to you, threatening the legacy of a family.

And this is the very thing that you, as his lady, can help your husband guard against. A wife can potentially cripple a man, or she can catapult him towards a more abundant life. She can point him toward making a stronger commitment to serving Christ, helping him strive for greater integrity. She can give him the safety to express his tender side and help him discover his natural male strength.

You, more than any other person in your husband's life, can know his deepest needs: the quiet longing of his soul…his search for significance…his frailties, weaknesses that he can hide from others but never from you…his God-given strengths, making you proud of his victories.

You can help him…or hurt him. God has placed you strategically to help equip him, to strongly influence him, to help shape and mold his life.

A great deal of a man's personal success and right choices, I believe, can be traced to the woman who whispers into his ear at night. He is naturally open to the one who holds the key to his heart. I do not mean to imply that a man turns control of his destiny over to his wife; he does not. He remains responsible for his thoughts, his words, his life choices, and his actions. But he is vulnerable to his wife and her ways. As a good friend (and the pastor who married Gary and me) once said, a bad woman can break her man and a good woman can make him better.

Once I met a woman who appeared lovely from a distance, but by getting closer and talking with her I saw a different side. She seemed about the most critical woman I had ever met. Her words were negative and bitter, and void of kindness. She was critical of her children, critical of her home, critical of her hairstyle and her lifestyle…but mostly she was critical of her man. I started feeling quite uncomfortable, and wanted to excuse myself from her presence. Deep down I was thinking, *Here is a deeply wounded woman who has become a bitter, wounding wife.*

As a young man, her husband had been known for being lighthearted and fun. Those who knew him best described him as being committed to his family and loyal to his wife. But years of her chronic criticism took their toll. He had become depleted of his valor and masculinity. In later years his condition became even sadder.

He was vulnerable to his wife. She held within her reach the very keys to his heart, but her inability to recognize his worth eventually wasted his inner person away.

In your mind's eye, look ahead: What will *your* knight look like after the next five years of being exposed to you?

You can know this for sure: Much of his success in guarding his heart will not be achieved unless you are at his side. His conquest in the raging battle he faces will greatly depend on your womanly response to him as a man.

> An excellent wife, who can find?
>> For her worth is far above jewels.
> The heart of her husband trusts in her,
>> and he will have no lack of gain.
> She does him good and not evil
>> all the days of her life. (Proverbs 31:10-12)

The Seven Keys

Now let's take a look at these seven keys to understanding your man. You may see that only a few of them represent your experience in marriage. Or this list may be a clean sweep, with all of them hitting home.

I'd like to start with perhaps your husband's greatest need of all: to be *honored* by you.

KEY 1

Honoring Him and His World

Now let me show you specific ways to help your knight prepare for the battle at hand by honoring him and his world. Let me unveil for you how your presence in your husband's life—your attitudes, your responsiveness, your unique qualities—can nurture and unleash the very strength he needs in fighting this never ending war.

Help Him Achieve His Visions

Deep inside every man is a boy and his dreams.

Close your eyes for a moment and envision your husband as a sure-footed, energetic, clear-thinking, twinkle-eyed ten-year-old with bounce in his step, taking a shot at some baskets—in love with life! His future was nothing short of promising. It's certain he had great plans.

If you could go back to that time, what are the fresh and untainted dreams your husband would share from his heart?

Now picture him in the years when he first entered young manhood. What were the dreams he had in those days, dreams unmarred by the pain of future disappointments or the reality of survival?

And now, think of him as he is today. Has he quit dreaming? If so, when did it happen, and why? Should a man ever quit dreaming? I don't think so.

How often have you walked into a man's office and noticed the display of awards, diplomas, trophies, and photographs of himself with the people who are important in his life? These all reflect a message to himself: "I'm really doing okay." A man's dreams and his search for his identity are closely intertwined with what he *does*. So he often surrounds himself with the outward signs of his accomplishments.

Men derive an enormous amount of their self-esteem from their life work. They are just wired that way. They expect this work to be hard at times. This is in keeping with Genesis 3, where God promised Adam toilsome work all the days of his life. (It seems that God meant what He said—as He generally does!)

As women, we need to recognize that the satisfaction a man is capable of achieving from his work, coupled with the time it requires of him, can potentially consume him. Pressures from a tough world besiege him. It's staggering what men have to put up with. A man is told to work harder and to produce more and more…because there's someone right behind him who can always take his place.

Many times I talk to women whose husbands are faced with the possibility of a planned or unplanned career change. Often a woman can get so preoccupied with the security of their present income that she doesn't consider what opportunities the change could hold for her husband, apart from a salary cut and starting over. For him to take another job would cause her to experience the loss of financial security, possibly leaving her to feel out of control with life.

But ask yourself this question: If taking a salary cut would bring your husband a sense of purpose, allowing him to find enjoyment in life and ulti-mately pushing him closer to God, then wouldn't it be worth it? A man can learn some of his greatest spiritual lessons by depending on God to provide—rather than on his own ability to bring in his income.

My mind goes back several years to the time when Gary was a full-time student in graduate school, as well as the full-time director of a correctional facility. Once his schooling was complete, the day soon came when he and I began seriously mulling over the idea of making a major career change: opening up a private practice counseling office.

I was overwhelmed by all the responsibilities and changes the transition represented. But as we prayed together as a married couple, we began to experi-ence a real peace and conviction about the decision. We knew the change would be hard. It would not be without cost. Gary worked night and day in anticipa-tion of the extra expenses. When he wasn't working he was meeting with local physicians, pastors, and representatives of private and corporate businesses, informing them of the services he could provide.

In the midst of this transition, my dad one day came to visit. He made a peppery inquiry as to why we would want to leave behind the benefits we had enjoyed—guaranteed income, paid vacations and holidays, and insurance benefits for the whole family. It was fair for him to be asking such questions—he knew first-hand what he was talking about. He had successfully fought the "hand-to-mouth" battle of owning his own business while raising children and paying the never-ending influx of bills.

I listened intently to this golden-hearted dad of mine. He was looking out for us. But in my heart of hearts, I knew God had given Gary an incredible opportunity to use his gifts and talents for God's glory. And He had given us just enough measure of faith to follow His leading.

I attempted to explain this to Dad. Still, he felt uncertain for us. My final words to him were these: "Dad, we have got to follow God on this one." Through his life, my father had taught me much about boundaries, and being tough-minded enough to stick to them. There was no gray area: only black and white, right and wrong.

A few months ago, my parents toured our newly remodeled counseling offices. Watching their expressions, I saw how proud they were of Gary. Then I looked into my dad's face and remembered those words from a bygone era: *Dad, we need to follow God on this one.*

And we have followed Him. Our story is that of one young man's dream, a dream propelled by the grace of the same God who continues to put "wings" to dreams today.

Gary is the kind of man who is committed to one goal: liberating the people he comes into contact with on a daily basis. He liberates them by letting them know God's grace is available to each and every one of them. Part of Gary's purpose in this world is to take this very joy and to pass it on to other men. Hoarding him to myself, causing him to meet my needs exclusively, would be like capturing him for my own selfish gain. Under those conditions, neither one of us would be happy. It would be a loss if Gary could not achieve God's purpose for him in the lives of other men.

Are you willing to release your man, allowing him to fulfill the plans God has for him? What is it that your man is called to do with his life? How can he better serve God? How are you strategically counseling your husband? Do your ideas and opinions benefit him, or are you pulling him into a different direction to meet only your needs?

How can you help your husband to take risks so he isn't filled with regret later? How can you come alongside and release him into actualizing a career dream that will bring real satisfaction and meaning to his life when he is stirred to follow God in a career move?

First: Be prayerful. Pray individually, and meet as a couple to pray jointly. Career changes, even in their mildest form, can impose a lot of stress on the family at large. Often it's you, his wife, who will pick up the slack. The doubled stress load can add a lot of weight to those shoulders of yours; count the stress-factor up front.

Second: Be alert to whatever brings joy back into his life. Ask yourself: Do my husband's training and skills line up with his life goals, his dreams, and his natural talents? Are there opportunities for him to use his gifts in his present position? Would achieving such opportunities entail a move? Can I, as his wife, provide the relational, emotional, and financial support system needed to back up his goals?

Third: If he doesn't have the degree to get into his career of choice, ask yourself how you can help him acquire it without sacrificing your marriage and family in the process. It was not easy for us when Gary returned to school to receive his doctoral degree, but going into the program we fully recognized this. Early on, we prayed earnestly together for direction. We knew the Lord was leading us to make that decision. There were times of real sacrifice for all of us in our family. But we continuously sought God's counsel.

In fact, I can now say we learned lessons that would last for a lifetime. Remember this: God doesn't promise that the road will be easy, but He does promise to give us the strength necessary to follow His will for our lives. What incredible assurance!

Believe in Him

In their book *Rocking the Roles,* Robert Lewis and William Hendricks write,

> A man has two significant mirrors in his life: one is his work, the other is his wife. Looking into them, he asks important questions of identity, worth, and meaning. Both will reflect back to him strong messages about his manhood. Over time, what he receives from them will spell the difference between a life of satisfaction and a life of deep frustration.

They go on to say,

> Of the two, you as a woman are the most important over a lifetime in helping your man feel good about himself. Why? Because there are times when work is just work. And there will be times when he has no work. But he will want you there, energizing and stabilizing his life.

I am convinced that the most important way of demonstrating my support in Gary's life is to launch him daily with my genuine belief in him as a man. *Belief.* One short six-letter word. But how many common, ordinary men have been groomed for knighthood by someone who cared enough to send them out the door each day with a renewed belief in their mission in life? Such belief can stir up embers that have died out in his heart and refuel the fire of passion for life.

Are you expressing that belief? Or are you passively uninterested and unin-
volved in your husband's interests and dreams?

Encourage your knight to follow his dreams. Do you know what those
dreams are? Get involved with his world. Listen to what he is struggling with at
work. And listen to the silences…what he's not opening up about. These can be
key to understanding where he may feel some sense of fear or stress in his life.

Right now he may be longing for timely words of your belief in him: "Go
for it…I believe in you and what you are doing…Give it a try!" Give your
husband your heartfelt belief. He needs it to succeed as a man.

Respect Him

Ultimately, your man wants respect and the support of his own wife. With your
confidence planted in his heart, he can face potentially any trial that comes his
way. When you verbalize your respect of him, your words act as a stimulus and
are a major source of encouragement in his life!

Life and death are in the power of words. (Proverbs 18:21)

Without your support, he will never feel fully successful as a man.
Unexpressed respect or lack of respect can leave a man lost and forgotten, and in
time, bitterness will settle in. Critical remarks will act as a depressant and
discourage him. How many homes today resemble graveyards resulting from
emotional deaths that were caused by words used in the home?

Encourage Him

Encouragement. Never take this word lightly. It literally means "to give courage."
Offering words that express your belief in someone can be like throwing him a
life preserver while he's drowning in the sea of despair. Encouragement is life-
changing. It empowers another person to take that risk or that big step. It can
keep him on the right track so he can continue to serve God, his family, and his
world.

A key time for encouragement in our home is at the end of the workday.
Gary just loves to be greeted when he arrives home. I must confess, there have
been times when I've heard him come in and thought, *If only I could get one*

more chore done…then I'll be finished with my list. I would ignore his entrance, and our relationship ended up suffering later. He felt it, and so did I.

We've learned that the best way to tune into each other at the end of the work day is for Gary and I to go into the living room, listen to the matters that are on each other's hearts, and encourage one other. This is one way we slow down and find balance in our lives.

Instead of criticizing him, make your man your very best friend by carving out time to share his emotional load.

Your husband's development (or lack of it) can result from many different factors in his life. He's a product of his family background, his life experiences, and his interactions with his friends and business associates. But the atmosphere of the home, which includes verbal and nonverbal communication, has been key in shaping his identity and behavior. And many men come from families that were hard on them.

Your husband may have experienced years of relentless critical remarks and may still be harboring much of that pent-up hurt today. How does it come out? Usually in some form of anger. Is he critical of your every move? Does it seem like you never do anything right? What you're hearing is a "tape" of the type of words he grew up with in his home. Each time he becomes hurt, discouraged, or frustrated, that inner tape goes off again. The words are echoes from his past: "You're no good! You aren't going to amount to anything! If only you were more like your brother! You are a failure!" No one gets over that kind of hurt overnight.

Listen closely, as you have the opportunity to relive this man's past, to see him as a young, impressionable, love-hungry boy. Your man continues to need you, especially if he has carried this burden of belittlement for a lifetime. He may not always act like it, but there is great worth in your kind and encouraging words to him; they can build up his self-worth.

Sometimes a woman's role is to come alongside her man and help him reprogram that lousy tape. Help your husband by "re-recording" your voice over those voices of the past, changing the message to words of genuine belief and encouragement.

As a woman, I choose daily what I will make an issue of and what I'm willing to walk away from. As Robert Louis Stevenson said, "Make the most of the best and the least of the worst." Far too often I end up making "the most" of "the worst." You do your husband enormous good when you authentically validate him by *telling* him what he does right. As his need for encouragement is fulfilled, in time he'll replace that old tape with your genuine appraisal of what he does right.

Where do you begin? By proactively demonstrating that you love your husband. You may need help in uncovering his strengths, his personal interests, or uniqueness. Rediscovering things about him you have overlooked for years can bring new excitement back into the marriage. How can you go about detecting these hidden qualities?

First of all: Study your husband. Watch for what makes his eyes brighten. Make it your goal to know him better than he knows himself.

Second: Listen to your husband. Give him your complete attention, even if you don't have a clue to what he's talking about. Ask questions. Listen to his voice as he speeds up talking when he is excited; find out what it means when he slows way down. Notice how he carefully chooses his words when they touch on a subject close to his heart. You will learn about what he is thinking about, what his focus is, what is important in his life, and what he is giving himself to. You connect as a couple when you give him your undivided attention.

Third: Show him you appreciate him. Praise him for his character qualities, the wisdom he shows in making tough decisions. He can't read your mind; make sure you tell him what he did right. Think about his very character as a man, his ability to be loyal, the way he honors you, his sense of humor, his achievements in the work force, his ability to start a project and complete it, his leadership qualities, and his personal aspirations.

Express your love for the convictions that he has stood by in his family, in his church, and in his career. It's a tough world out there. You don't always have to agree with him on some of those decisions he has made, but you can praise him for having the courage it takes to stand by them.

Finally, ask yourself, "What kind of tape am I playing in *my* headset?" The tapes we play in our own minds help determine our words and actions.

In Philippians 4:8, Paul reminds us to program our own minds with thoughts that are based in truth—thoughts that are "noble, right, pure, lovely, admirable, excellent, and praiseworthy." Do those words describe your thoughts? Or are you thinking critical thoughts? What kind of tape have you got going in there?

Read God's Word and ask God to help you change from criticizing to encouraging that man of yours. For the effect your words can have on him is nothing short of amazing.

KEY 2

Watching Out for Sabotage

You are a pillar of power in your husband's life. But if this power is misman-aged, you can deeply wound your knight.

You have the potential of being like Delilah with Samson. Despite all his physical strength, her persistence wore him down. He was no match for her. We, too, can aid in the ultimate unraveling of God's plans for the lives of our men, taking our men down. We can sabotage our husband's growth even while we're ignorant of—or blind to—the ways in which we're doing it.

Just for starters, here's a list of some of the ways women are sabotaging their marriages today.

The Desire to Control

For some women, the sabotage is an attempt to capture and dominate their husbands. Such action only robs men of their ability to become all God called them to be. Men aren't meant to be captured. To do so is to pull them down, diminish their manhood, and hold them hostage.

Don't make the error of running around with your "Junior Holy Spirit" badge pinned on, intending to manipulate your husband into becoming someone he isn't. We're only acting selfishly when we lay those unmet expecta-tions on our men. Accept your husband the way he is, this minute.

In one way or another, the selfish woman gives her husband negative ultimatums. Her motto is "My way or nothing!" It's a belittling attitude that she can't afford to have.

Distractions

The distracted woman is preoccupied with the opportunities life brings her way —and which steal time and attention away from her husband. Whether she has a career or works in the home full-time, distractions keep her focused on every "good" thing that comes along, either outside or inside her home. Eventually these things take priority over her husband.

What kind of activities (good causes, of course) are you giving your life to? Women often build their careers, attend club meetings, and carpool their children from one activity to another. They volunteer, decorate their homes, work out at fitness centers, and buy more and more things that eventually land at the yearly garage sale or in the lap of the Salvation Army.

Your daily choices can either build your marriage or erode it. What will your marriage look like in the next five years? Your thoughts, attitudes, and actions all contribute to, or detract from, the intimacy of your marriage relationship. Are you keeping your husband in focus; do you continue to enjoy him?

Above all else, concentrate on those desires that will keep you on the right path. Put boundaries on your affections; don't go after everything you see. Distractions have a way of cluttering up our time, energy, and calendars, keeping us so overloaded that we aren't able to complete any task with a sense of joy and fulfillment. What do you expect to gain from being involved in so many different activities? Are you attempting to be the super-wife, while in reality you're simply draining yourself of your best energy?

Are you giving a steady diet of "emotional leftovers" to the man you promised to love and cherish? Or is he still the most important person in the world to you? Is too much busyness keeping your relationships with your husband and children at an acquaintance level? A distracted wife can unintentionally kill the relational intimacy in her marriage.

Comparison

The weapon Satan seems to use most in relationships is comparison. This lethal weapon is guaranteed to strike the target of his heart. Through comparison, you can place your unmet expectations on your husband over and over again.

Have you ever thought how easy it is to respect someone you hardly even know—professional associates, doctors, pastors, and many other strangers? At ninety yards, anybody can look really good. Meanwhile the people we love most, the ones who most need our belief in them, don't receive our respect.

Stay away from comparison. Your husband can be hurt by any statement that would even mildly suggest that you respect any other man more than you respect him. He probably will never discuss openly how this comparison impales his very manhood. But be assured that he needs you to keep him positioned exclusively as *your man,* and proud of it.

Three Sure-Fire Ways to Bring Him Down

1. Assume He Knows Your Mind—We often assume men are 'mind readers' who automatically understand the way we feel. Nothing could be further from the truth. Men need specific information and instructions from us so they can better understand us.

2. Focus on His Weakness—If you really want to inflict injury on your husband, expose his weaknesses in public. Nothing can hurt him more. And though he won't let anyone know it, he takes much longer to recover on the inside than a woman.

Deep inside every grown man is a little boy who, if treated with respect and given genuine encouragement and affirmation, will respond and grow. Our husbands look to us for emotional signals, and we give those signals very naturally. Women are the nurturers; we affirm, and cheer our men on. A good cheerleader knows she's cheering for a winner! Without even realizing it, our husbands look to us to answer the unspoken question: "How am I doing as a man?"

3. Criticize Him—How do you respond when your husband puts in a long day at work? Does he come home to nagging? Proverbs 25:24 was written a long time ago, but maybe you know a 1990s woman like this: "Better to live on a corner of the roof than share a house with a quarrelsome woman." Instead of nagging, we need to be sensible. Replace your natural inclination to challenge your husband, which can come across as criticism, with the attitude of encouragement.

KEY 3

Love Him Unconditionally

A wise, older woman once explained the difference between love and infatuation in this way: "Infatuation is when you think he's as sexy as Tom Cruise, as smart as Albert Einstein, as witty as David Letterman, and as athletic as Joe Montana. Love is when you realize he's as sexy as Albert Einstein, as athletic as David Letterman, as witty as Joe Montana, and nothing like Tom Cruise…but you'll take him anyway!"

Why do we place such a high standard on our men at times? Ruth Graham once said, "Only Jesus can be Jesus." Amen, Ruth. That statement speaks to me as a wife. Each of us needs to appreciate her husband as a person, regardless of his strengths and weaknesses. True love is not performance-based.

Real love means accepting your husband for who he is, and not comparing him to, or defining him by, some phantom image. Such judgment isn't fair to him and will only drive him away from you. Your marriage must be girded in unconditional love.

Love him for who he is today. Love him with all his imperfections—in spite of his flaws, and even his failures. God can use those very characteristics to propel him into a deeper, more connected relationship with Him. Jesus Christ is the One who is shaping your husband into the man he has yet to become. It is crucial that you honor your man; you don't dare sabotage the refinement process going on in his life. That's why it's imperative to love our husbands unconditionally. By withholding love from your husband, you potentially interfere with the delicate growth process going on in his heart.

Why is unconditional love so important? Because it mirrors the very love Christ had for us. While we were in a sinful state, full of guilt and shame, Christ died on the cross for every one of our sins. *That* is unconditional love. It is the very love that was modeled at the cross, the kind of love that accepts me just as I am.

Is your love for your husband unconditional? Or do you watch his every move with a critical eye? Do you keep any "conditions" in the middle of your marriage? Do you place the expectations for your relationship so high that disaster is inevitable?

Compare your love for your husband with the love described in 1 Corinthians 13. Are you patient and kind? Or are you envious and proud? Do you keep records of your husband's wrongs, then bring them out at a time that's advantageous for you? Do you continue bringing things up that should have been over and dealt with long ago? God knows that a person who hangs on too tightly to such things will ultimately destroy herself. By attempting to keep her man in bondage, she will, in fact, find herself a slave to her list of resentments.

When your love is unconditional, you care enough to talk through the issues at hand, release the offense, and genuinely love the offender. That is the rare beauty of unconditional love: You are able to replace the hurt with genuine love and forgiveness.

Women, by their very nature, have an incredible capacity to nurture relational intimacy. We are as gentle gardeners in an imperfect, dry, parched world that's in need of water; it is through women that this cool refreshment of real love can be dispensed. This kind of nurturing can rejuvenate a marriage relationship.

Every one of us longs to be loved with no strings attached. We ache for acceptance that comes with no pressure to perform: love that requires no letters of achievement behind our last names. Your husband longs for the freedom to be fully who he is, guaranteed that his dearest wife will stand beside him through it all. He cherishes the pride of knowing you believe in him, regardless of the cost.

If your mate hasn't fully experienced this ultimate kind of love, he may try —like a naughty kid—to prove whether you *really* love him just the way he is. He may act up at times to test the level of your commitment to him, without openly verbalizing what he is doing. He is most likely blind to the need that is driving him to behave in this extreme manner.

Commitment involves being deeply and passionately proud of the man you stand joined with. If you do not love your husband for all he is, you are leaving him vulnerable and your marriage unguarded.

An unyielding, unwavering commitment to your husband *regardless* of the circumstances, coupled with unconditional love, can mend a lot of the soul's broken fences. It produces genuine healing for the wounded man.

Allow Him to Be Needed by You

Your husband's number one need as a man is to be needed by you. Every morning I wake up to these gently whispered words, "Barb, I need you." These are words from a man's soul, four words that encompass the most vulnerable point of our relational world. Those words connect Gary and me each morning.

Your husband needs you, too. Unfortunately, he may not know how to verbalize his need of you. (He's a guy, remember?) That need may remain unspoken, but the need is ever there.

Gary and I have traveled across the United States and spoken to thousands of couples about marriage. On one particular occasion, I spoke to a woman who managed and ran a family business with her husband. She was sharp—bright, attractive, and loaded with talent.

She and her husband had known each other since they were kids. They had gone to school together, married, and had three kids at home. Sadly, she shared that although she had worked hard, she had neglected her husband's need to be needed. A female employee had "stepped in" to meet that need. Wrongly, his guard was down and the employee had violated his boundary by crossing over that fine line. She had started by complimenting him on his broad shoulders, then she stepped up to become his advocate, his cheerleader.

Your husband has a strong need to be needed. Do your best to meet that need. Ignoring it won't make it go away. Don't let any other woman step into your position and become your husband's cheerleader. You might imagine an absolute fox luring and charming your man. Reality indicates that she doesn't have to be. Many times, another woman simply has her eye out for a *vulnerable* man, one whose guard against enemy invasion is down—a man left needy and unattended. This kind of woman can spot him a mile away, and she's learned only too well how to demonstrate her need for him.

> For the lips of an adulteress drip honey,
>> and her speech is smoother than oil. (Proverbs 5: 3)

Love him. Be the lady of one knight—your knight.

KEY 4

Understanding Your Differences

Yes, men and women are different. But sometimes we women become angry with men. We want them to want what we want. We want them to feel the way we feel. We falsely assume that men should behave just like us because they are made just like us. But I tell you they're not. Our husbands are one-hundred percent man. And because we don't have an ounce of masculinity in us, we need to pay close attention to how they think. We need to understand their unique characteristics. By fully accepting our differences, we can learn to love and enjoy each other's companionship.

You've probably heard of many of the common differences observed between men and women: In general, men are more solution-oriented, more logical and less emotional, less verbal, and more single-focused. A man tends to view himself by what he does, what he owns, his hobbies and his titles, while a woman thinks more in terms of relationships. The list goes on and on.

Every couple is a unique set of these male/female differences, but the differences are always there. That's why even if you feel you and your husband are ideally matched, you need to become a student of the man you married; otherwise resentment is sure to build. The more you understand your husband's male characteristics, the more you can access his deep need for you in his life and begin to meet those needs intimately.

So study your man. Listen to him. Communicate with him. Ask him what his greatest needs are. Your attitude is the most important component of the relationship. It's easy to appreciate sameness. It is much harder to esteem differences.

Communicate Openly with Him

Sometimes when I get upset about something, I pull in and stop talking, instead of telling Gary specifically what's bothering me. Our conversation may go something like this:

"What's wrong?"

"Nothing!" Actually, I'm thinking, *Surely you've must know. The handwriting is on the wall; the evidence is as plain as day. Can't you figure out what's bothering me?*

Truthfully, ladies, he can't. We assume men think like us, but they don't. Stay away from double messages. Don't make the mistakes I have. Tell your husband honestly what you are thinking and feeling. As a woman, I constantly need to be alert to the way in which I communicate with my man, and not assume he already has it figured out.

And when he is talking, work on giving your husband your undivided attention. He needs you to listen to him. If you don't, you will never know him intimately.

Give your man time to figure out his feelings. He generally takes longer to process them. As a man, he is more logical. Allow time for his thoughts to get from his head down to his heart, and then form into words. Work on creating a safe environment in which your man can express himself. Remember that real love always allows room for differing styles of communication and differing ways to process. The goal is to discover a process through which he can share his hopes, his dreams, and his failures, knowing he will still be accepted.

I believe strongly that women are, without a doubt, their husbands' greatest teachers when it comes to the expression of thoughts. We can tap into well-springs of emotions that may have lain dormant for years. You hold the key of love which can unlock this facet of your husband.

Can you describe your husband and yourself as soul-mates? Even if you can't now, someday down the road you may. What a wonderful gift it is to call your husband your best friend.

A worthy wife is her husband's joy and crown. (Proverbs 12:4)

Tenderly Touch Him

The time was 9:00 A.M. on the button, on a cold and rainy day. I stood shivering by my desk at Gary's office. As his partner in life, I went in one day each week to help out with different projects. On this particular day, I had just arrived after running our two girls to school. I was ready to give Gary my best.

His door opened to his office as he heard me enter. Now keep in mind that he had been up since five o'clock, and counseling since seven. To him it seemed like mid-morning.

"Barb," I heard him say. "Could you please step into my office? There are a few things I need to go over with you."

Oh, great, I thought. *Here comes The List.*

The List greeted me every Friday morning when I went to work. Sometimes Gary acted like a dog on point over this list of "must do's." Did he realize that he had done this to me every week for ten years?

Oh, well...

I walked into his office. Gary seemed more intense than usual. He tends to become increasingly more business-like when he's stressed, and that day was no exception.

"Please come over to my desk," he said, "and I'll go through this with you." I stood behind him and looked at the piece of paper he held. On it were at least twenty-seven items that needed my attention...all before noon!

As usual, Gary began talking through The List. The more he covered, the more tension I heard in his voice.

Poor guy, I thought. *It's only nine and he's already in hyper-drive.*

I leaned into him from behind and naturally put my hands on his shoulders, which were stiff from carrying his work load. As he continued to read, I began to gently massage his shoulders and neck and back.

Then something totally unprecedented happened: *He stopped reading The List.*

In tune with his silence, his body started to relax. That "bird dog" had lost his point! He was really beginning to loosen up as I continued working on those shoulders.

Then I stepped back, took the list from his hand, thanked him for going over it with me...and I was outta there!

Then something else unprecedented happened: That morning he made at least three different—and unnecessary—trips into my office. He was more relaxed than usual—winking at me, smiling. Why, I could hardly get my work done with him around so much!

Touch. It seems like a fairly light-weight word, doesn't it? Yet touch acts as a "defining moment" in your mate's memory. He hears your spoken words, but touch relays the message with genuine warmth. It helps him to feel happy and truly cared for.

Every marriage needs lots of healthy and appropriate touch. That need can be met through hugs, pats on the back, even a back rub at the end of a day. Touch helps men to feel loved and worthy. When you are giving your man this kind of blessing, you are protecting him from temptations in the world by meeting one of his greatest needs. A woman, by her very nature, has the ability to teach her husband about the importance of tenderness in touch.

Understand His Sexual Needs

She stood awkwardly, waiting for me. I barely caught her out of the corner of my eye. I had just finished giving a women's seminar, and several women were lining up to talk with me. We had covered a myriad of topics about marriage that morning, and they had sparked a lot of interest from the women. The gals were fired-up and pretty chatty. But this one, young, twenty-something woman hung back, patiently waiting for me to finish answering the others' questions.

After everyone was gone she hesitantly approached me. She said she had been married for about two years. Then, taking a deep breath, she mustered up enough courage to talk about a topic that is delicate for all of us as women. She began to confide:

"I've never breathed this to anyone before, but when my husband and I have been apart and he returns home from a business trip, the first thing he wants to do is to take me to the bedroom. He can't keep his hands off me.

"I have the hardest time adjusting to him returning home because all I want is to emotionally connect to this man and talk with him about everything that has gone on in his absence. But he seems to have his mind on just one thing, and that one thing is sex. I've been wearing so many hats, my mind on just about everything…but that! I just don't understand why he's like that. It's causing me a great deal of stress. He just doesn't seem to want to communicate. I don't get it. Why is he like that?"

What a great question! The scene just described probably sounds familiar to scores of women. Sexually, men are clearly wired differently than women, but that doesn't make them "weird" or wrong. They are just distinctively male! Masculinity contrasts femininity. We all know we don't want men who act like women. But we desperately desire men who are sensitive to our needs.

No matter how compatible you are as a couple, you need to address the foundational issue: He is a man. Not only does he look like a man, but he thinks like one. And sex is very important to him. Sex is a viable means for a man to communicate and express himself with his wife; he exposes his deepest sense of masculinity in his most vulnerable state. Much of a man's self-esteem is enhanced during his most intimate moments with you, his wife.

To your husband, sex is a means of communication and an attempt to become one with you spiritually, emotionally, and physically. In fact, sex can be the barometer of how things are going in other areas of your relationship. When there have been times of good communication and healthy growth in your relationship, you tend to celebrate by spending time alone together.

In cases of unresolved conflict, it's a smart man who takes the time to work out these issues with his wife! It is difficult for a woman to transcend the points that divide her and her husband. To women, it just makes sense that there should be some order in the relationship before physical intimacy can be experienced. We see sex not as an event, but as a whole-life orientation.

If your husband has been busy and distracted, if he has not maintained the relationship, frankly, you won't be interested. Men aren't generally as sensitive to those basic relational dynamics, but they remain some of the most meaningful avenues of deep connection between husband and wife. The man doesn't speak the same language as does his counterpart; his message is more condensed to basically two words: "Anytime. Anywhere!" We *are* different!

The truth is that a man's ego is as fragile as an eggshell. You, his wife, have a tremendous opportunity to communicate within the confines of your relationship how truly worthy he is. So many men long to be affirmed by their wives in this exclusive relationship. Many men cry out silently to their wives, "Am I worthy in your eyes? Am I doing okay as a man?" You can affirm him within the safety of your exclusive relationship.

The typical man worries a lot about how his bride will receive him. Will she scorn his advances? Will she passively put up with them until they've stopped?

Or will she receive him with joy? I don't think any woman fully understands how powerful are her responses. When you receive your mate with a heart full of joy, you can actually build into him a sense of worth, causing him to feel desirable and acceptable.

In *To Have and to Hold,* Jo Renich writes, "There is more to building your mate's self-esteem in the bedroom than what you see. His very confidence is on the line. Sex can be a source of rejection, and a wrong attitude can really cut into the heart of your husband." Your response to his initiation of sex is paramount in setting the tone for your time as a couple. You may ask yourself this question: "Does my husband really sense my sexual attitude?"

Listen to the words of Song of Solomon 7:10-12.

> I am my beloved's and his desire is for me.
> Come, my beloved, let us go out in the country,
>   let us spend the night in the villages.
> Let us rise early and go to the vineyards…
> There I will give you my love.

Do you hear the excitement in her voice? This woman was delighted to be alone with her man! You don't hear any whining: "Do we *have* to?" This woman knows she is married to a winner, and she is smart enough to express it within the exclusive bonds of marriage.

Look Your Best

This morning while I was getting my hair cut, I browsed through the magazines in search of something readable. Some women's magazines blast their covers with images of super-models who are so gorgeous, I can't begin to relate to them. But comparison took it's jaundiced course. Mirrors plastered the salon from wall to wall. Without thinking, I looked up from those pages, and was faced with the reflection in that mirror.

Any woman whose hair has been foiled, wrapped, highlighted, pulled or permed, or who has donned the basic wet-head look, would understand: I looked nothing short of frightful! I paled in comparison to those models.

Choosing to bypass further torture, I put down the magazine and opted for a *Ladies' Home Journal.* I scanned the index of monthly features and my eyes fell upon an article on beauty tips that can help us 'look good.' Believe me, at that point I was very interested! It looked safe enough, and I opened to the page and read along. Now, something in the article really hooked me. It wasn't in the 'how to' section. It wasn't the technique or application. No, it wasn't the way Kathie Lee glues her nails or conceals her shadows. It was in the way the article ended: "…and Frank loves the way I look!"

Think about it: Your best friend gets her hair cut, you notice. Your mom gets some new jewelry, you take notice. Your daughter buys a new sweater, it catches your eye. But a man is visually "on point" almost all the time. He is visually alert and is especially attracted to beauty. Beauty leaves an indelible impression in his mind's eye, and women are beautiful creatures.

What keeps a man captivated in his marriage? Does a woman need to look like an absolute knock-out twenty-four hours a day? All day long a man encounters beautifully dressed and attractive women. What does he encounter when he walks in the house at night? Sometimes you look pretty good, and then there are other times…. Well, we all have them.

Perhaps you have been married a while and you're taking each other for granted. The newness wears off and you get acclimated to each other. Eventually, you quit trying so hard to look good for your husband. I caution you not to take up residency on the 'isle of denial.' Men will always be creatures of vision, whether women understand this or not. How can you help your man guard his heart? Stay alert for ways to look attractive for your husband. There are countless ways to improve your appearance. Your man needs you to take care of yourself. There are sharp and beautiful women all around us; they are the very women who remind us not to become dull in our appearance.

KEY 5

Honoring His Friendships

Encourage your husband to spend time with like-minded men. Men are pace-setters, and leadership qualities need to be reinforced. Men need to go through life with other men who desire to follow Jesus Christ regardless of the cost. They need to sharpen each other as "iron sharpens iron."

Men need male friends who will point them to God; this is essential if they are going to avoid life's assaults. They need like-minded men who are willing to walk that road with one another…men who are willing to challenge each other and hold each other accountable.

As a wife, I like that. It makes me feel safe to realize Gary has caring, concerned men in his life who love him.

Be His Friend

Our husbands not only need their male friendships; they also need us to be their friends as well.

Someone once gave me a card that read: "What women want: To be loved, to be listened to, to be desired, to be respected, to be needed, to be trusted, and sometimes just to be held. What men want: Tickets to the World Series!" Discover your husband's interests, and then do something truly mad: join him in them!

In *His Needs, Her Needs,* Willard Harley says that it's imperative for marriage partners to experience their most enjoyable recreational moments with each other. He says, "After marriage, a wife often tries to interest her husband in activities more to her liking. If her attempts fail, she may encourage her husband to continue his recreational activities without her. That is a dangerous option, because men place a surprising importance on having their wife as a recreational companion."

While I was at lunch with friends the other day, one woman mentioned that her husband had found a "boating buddy." Our "recreation expert" at the table exclaimed, "Girl, *you* need to be his boating buddy!" (Hey, it wasn't me! I just sat there and took notes.) The woman continued to tell us how she plays in a volleyball league with her husband and works out with him at the gym. She went on to share that she even went hunting with him once.

"Did you shoot the gun?" we asked.

"No. I sat in the car as he walked the fields. We spent a great day riding in the country and just talking," she explained. One couple I know took up playing tennis together. The husband's response to his wife was, "This is what I always thought marriage would be like."

I know a number of women who golf with their husbands. Some great friends of ours just got a Harley Davidson, which they enjoy together. (Would you believe the wife bought it for her husband? What a woman! She's making the rest of us look pretty tame.)

Last weekend Gary dusted off and cleaned up my bicycle, and we ventured out on a path together. It was exhilarating! We relaxed, laughed, and awakened those endorphins. When we walked in, laughing, our kids didn't recognize us. We were greeted with, "Just where have you been and what have you been doing?" Their questions were answered by our smiles.

Couples need to participate in these kinds of activities together. This element of your relationship isn't negotiable; it's essential. This may mean a sacrifice of your time, and sometimes your interests, but it is a gift your husband will always cherish, and one that can draw you closer as a couple in a way nothing else can. Many women would give anything to go back to a time when they were invited to share in their husbands' fun. It is a privileged woman whose husband still gravitates towards her and desires her company.

Make sure your marriage is full of fun and laughter. It will remind your husband that he's married to the finest woman alive! Pleasure and relaxation together are the very things that pull couples together, and in the future will cause your grown-up children to want to come home to laugh together as a family again.

KEY 6

Clarifying Your Family Roles

God called woman a "helper" to man. Our culture tends to label a "helper" as someone second-rate. But not so in the Bible. The Hebrew word translated as "helper" equates to the English word "completer," and elsewhere in the Old Testament it's always used in reference to God Himself. It is a title of honor and great worth.

This leads us to a better understanding of a woman's distinctive strengths. It implies that by her very uniqueness, woman offers her husband life qualities that fully complete him, as no one else can. Think about it: When you need help in something, you go to someone who is stronger than you in that area, don't you? You seek assistance from someone who has capabilities beyond your own. We are often that "someone" for our husbands.

So what unique capabilities distinguish us in our husbands' lives?

A man generally knows *what* he wants, but on his own he doesn't always know how to appropriate the many parts of himself and arrive at his dreams. That's where we, as wives, can help our husbands discern what is right for them. That's the way we're made. It's all part of the original plan.

> The man said, "This is bone of my bones and flesh of my flesh;
> she shall be called 'woman,' for she was taken out of man."
> (Genesis 2:23)

God could have chosen to make woman from the dust of the ground, just as He had made man. But He did not. No, the woman was to have a unique entry into creation. She, like no other living creature, would be taken out of her partner, out of his very flesh and bones: made from his matter, matched with his heart. The woman was introduced to man at his side...and this is where she resides today.

As Mike Mason writes in *The Mystery of Marriage,*

> The Lord God made woman out of man's side and closed up the flesh, but in marriage He reopens this empty, aching place in a man and begins the process of putting the woman back in again, if not literally in the side, then certainly at it; permanently there, intrusively there, a sudden lifelong resident of a space which until that point the man will have considered to be his own private territory, even his own body. But in marriage he will cleave to the woman, and the woman to him, the way his own flesh cleaves to his own bones.

A woman generally offers a greater sensitivity than her counterpart. True, some men are more sensitive than others. But a woman has a distinctive understanding of unspoken messages. Some may venture to call it her "sixth" sense. Have you ever been conversing with your husband and your children when, almost like radar, you begin to pick up unspoken signals? Your child is communicating a few details, but you begin to sense far more—for you, as a woman, are alert to your child's inner spirit.

One day, Sarah came home from elementary school and was *too* quiet. She gave me a brief rundown of her day and slipped silently off to her room. My spirit left me uneasy. I knew in my heart there was more Sarah needed to share. Gary witnessed our conversation, but he didn't sense what I did. As we followed up on my hunch, we learned from Sarah that some girls at school had been pretty tough on her that day, and she was hurting.

God gave woman eyes that could peer into both her child's soul and her husband's heart. He gave woman ears that could hear the inaudible sounds of swelling tears that were never shed. Can I explain this innate gift God created in women? Not really. I just know it is real.

Our kids have a saying around our home: "Mom always finds out!" It may have started the time Missy got into the car after school and I looked at her and asked if she was going steady with a certain boy. Her reply was, "How did you know?"

Then I remember a time when Missy was staying overnight with a friend. Around 11:00 P.M. I felt a strong longing to call her. I really felt something was wrong. But I fought the urge to call—it was late, and I just wrote the feeling off to missing her. The next morning I learned that Missy had been in a car accident the night before. She was absolutely fine, but still my child needed her mommy.

A man often relies on logical reasoning rather than intuitive senses. The gift of sensitivity equips a woman to help her husband view a more complete picture. She has an inborn adeptness for developing relationships and desires deep, intimate communication—this gives her the perspective of viewing decisions based upon their impact on people and relationships, and helps her influence her man to be more people-centered instead of exclusively project-oriented.

The bottom line is that a helper is someone who enables a person to achieve something he is otherwise incapable of reaching on his own. You, your knight's lady—at his side and next to his heart—can more than anyone else help your husband to guard his precious heart and achieve his life dreams. The woman who completes her man is fulfilling her God-given design as a woman.

Let Him Be the Leader in Your Marriage

Our husbands may experience times of low self-esteem, feeling they just don't measure up. By transferring leadership from yourself to your husband, you can actually rebuild his self-esteem. Along with this transfer comes your release from the stress of wanting him to lead, but always having to have control.

Others have pointed out that a woman's need to control her husband often comes from a sense of insecurity. She believes wrongly that her identity and self-worth are derived from how well her husband behaves. She's assuming that *who she is* will be determined by something outside herself—her husband—rather than by God and her inner response to Him. Someone has put it well: "The fruit of the Spirit (in Galatians 5:23) is *self*-control, not *husband*-control."

I've watched too many men become passive because of women who lead the home. Release your husband to become all God has planned for him to be, as you become all God wants *you* to be. Know yourself so well, and respect yourself so much, that you can give to your husband the leadership of your home without hesitation.

The woman who truly respects her husband must also identify herself as valuable and significant. As she experiences the freedom to grow and to become all God has designed for her to be, her respect for her husband grows proportionately.

I want my husband to lead our home, but there are times when I want things *my* way! There's a power struggle going on inside of me. At times I think I could lead this home; it would be a breeze. But truthfully, it's too much for any woman to shoulder. When a woman is at the helm of her home, deep inside she is unhappy.

Women weren't created to lead the home. God didn't design the marriage relationship with the wife at the head of it.

We need to trust God and His plan. When we authentically choose to, He will show us how to lovingly submit to Him. We can demonstrate that same attitude of submissive love toward our husbands.

An excellent wife doesn't capture...she captivates.

Link Him with His Children

It was Father's Day: June 1966. I watched as my dad thanked each and every person for coming. Sadly, the event that brought everyone together had been a funeral. My dad, the only surviving child, had just buried his only remaining parent: the father who had always been his hero.

I sat alone in the back seat of our family car, feeling proud of my dad. He had been so kind and tender, and shown such regard for each of his father's friends. As the last car drove off down that gravel road, I saw my dad walk behind a bush. He stood there alone with his head in his hands. And in his anguish, he openly wept. It is a moment I will never forget.

When he was done, he pulled out a handkerchief, blew his nose, and got in the driver's seat to take his family of four back home.

As a twelve-year-old I thought, *How does a dad learn to be a man?* In that moment I had seen the child in my dad, and then watched as he—never missing a beat—stepped back into our lives as the dad who effectively led our family. What a man! Dad is still my hero.

As your husband attempts to become a mighty knight for God, it's vital not only that you keep him first in your heart, but that you keep him the hero to his children. Women are such nurturers, we have the natural ability to forge our husband and our children together. Give your husband your insight when your child is going through stress. Teach him to be more understanding, so he will be more patient with them.

Show him the key of entry into your child's world; teach him to cultivate childlike sensitivity. Your child will appreciate these efforts most of all. Your man doesn't dare risk using with his children the same, strong competitive side he is forced to use at work. If he did, they would fear the one man they need the very most. Teach your husband to be gentle with these moldable, pliable little people. He may not realize it, but the way he cares for them contributes to the development of their personalities.

Encourage your husband to spend time alone with each son or daughter. Your child deeply needs memories of "just Dad and me." Encourage your husband, for example, to take his child to work to demonstrate and explain what he does. Or when he runs an errand to the hardware store or takes the car for a fill-up, encourage him to take your child along. Some of life's best lessons can taught in the front seat of a car while driving down the street.

KEY 7

Committing Yourself to Him and to HIM

Make a commitment to be a Lady of one Knight. You may be thinking, *Barb, I did that on my wedding day.* But I challenge you to up the ante. The stakes have never been higher. The cost has never been higher to our families. I hope you aren't content to have a marriage that is just average; determine to experience a marriage that is stronger than all others, even one that could be classified as the absolute best. Such a marriage begins with a firm decision to stick by your man regardless of the cost. Make a commitment to be The Lady of One Knight!

Some women don't quite get the picture here. I think they get distracted—by other men. Unfortunately, they begin comparing their husband with other husbands. These women are the type who gaze longingly at the greener-looking grass on the other side of the fence. Their thoughts lure them beyond their own marriage.

"Her husband is *so* spiritual. He's the kind of man who leads his family. He brings home a good income. He's motivated to work! He's so handsome. He must work out"—and on and on. What happens to this person? She shifts her allegiance from her own husband to someone else's. She lives in an emotionally vulnerable state. Her position is precarious, as she isn't respecting the healthy boundaries of marriage. This gal could be a great friend to you, but she's dangerous to men because she emotionally attaches herself to them.

Where will her thoughts lead her after several years of wandering? What kind of toll will they take on the marriage and her children? Have you ever heard of an emotional affair? Whenever a woman gives her heart away, her emotions follow. Emotional wandering is just the dress rehearsal for the real show: a tangible violation of physical boundaries. Adultery.

A woman may be blinded by her emotions, thinking it could never happen to her. By the way, Satan helps to perpetuate that myth.

As women, we need to earnestly take every thought captive! Commit to being your husband's devoted wife! He needs you. This may be your chance to assist God in a real miracle: five years from now, who will your husband have become? Think of the challenge: Five years of an undying, unwavering, staunch commitment to your knight. Will he be stronger, yet increasingly more tender, because of the influence of your life?

Take my challenge: Be the lady of one—and only one—knight.

Focus on the Lord

Without a doubt, the most lasting key you give your husband is your rock-solid faith in following Jesus Christ. Keep the Living Lord present in your home. He is the Key to unlocking the treasure of your husband's heart. As a wife who holds within her reach the very key to her husband's heart, guard that key and look beyond to where our real strength comes from:

> He will be the sure foundation for your times, a rich store of salvation and wisdom and knowledge; the fear of the Lord is the key to the treasure. (Isaiah 33:6)

Your husband and family plug into you for a variety of needs. It is exhausting; there cannot be enough of you to go around unless you acquire strength from outside yourself. And our Lord promises to strengthen the weary, to increase the power of the weak. In fact, He says that those who put their hope in Him "will renew their strength. They will soar on wings like eagles; they will run and not grow weary, they will walk and not be faint" (Isaiah 40: 29-31).

As Hebrews 12:1 tells us, we're all running in a race before God and under the Lordship of Jesus Christ. As a woman and wife, how can you finish this race at your best, and how can you help your knight to finish well?

It is only through Christ that you can finish well, not growing weary and not losing heart. And through Him you also can help your husband finish well. You can have an incredible influence on his relationship with Christ.

Your man needs you as a soul-mate in following Christ. Open up your heart and share with your husband what you are learning. But as much as he counts on you, remember this: You cannot give what you do not have. You need to be working independently on your own relationship with Christ.

Our basic nature is so strongly tainted and depraved on its own, only the power of Christ can temper and change it. Only by nurturing our spirits through the reading of God's Word can we find lasting, fulfilling joy—joy that makes sense of our lives, leading us to live out God's ultimate plan, and impact those lives within our care. Such joy will keep you grounded. It is our only source of stability in this crazy world.

Read the Word. Get into a Bible study group with other women; draw from their experiences. An understanding of the very righteousness of God has a beautiful way of keeping our hearts guarded. Protected hearts are prepared to do battle with the enemy. A woman who finds her source of strength in Christ, who is ready and able to do what God requires of her, who is able to take risks, who knows she is liberated through Christ's shed blood at Calvary—such a woman is pretty incredible, wouldn't you say?

Pray about everything. Remember that with God, nothing is off limits. He's interested in the smallest areas of your life, and the biggest ones, too. Pray with your husband. Few experiences are as intimate as that of a husband and wife baring their souls before God and with one another.

Keep in stride with each other. I'm sure this is one of the reasons Paul addresses the issue of being "equally yoked." You both must have a burning passion to follow Christ at all costs. As you pursue God together as a couple, He can powerfully use you to impact your children, your friends, your parents, your community, and your world.

Of all the suggestions I've made about helping your husband to guard his heart, the one with the greatest impact is that of pointing him to Christ, whether he is a man who knows the living Lord through his own personal relationship or one who still needs to meet Him. Don't give up on your husband.

Just remember: Christ needs to be central to every decision you make. Remind your husband to take each thought captive before the Lord. You can give to your man in many different ways, but the most lasting gift is that of placing Christ in the middle of your marriage. Always remember: God can fulfill His purpose in your husband's life when you are at your man's side, strengthening and encouraging him. As your knight's lady, *you* have helped him to guard his heart!

And in the End...

Once more, gaze with me at a picture. Watch as your knight enters the presence of the living Lord.

Humbled, he approaches. Head down, eyes closed, he kneels at the feet of the King of kings.

Before you again is a vision of that treasure-filled, innermost chamber—your knight's heart. It is filled now with pure light, the glow of God himself. Your knight has kept his heart from evil. In purity he has followed the One he serves.

Then, like the crashing sound of a mighty roar, you hear the thundering of God's majestic voice:

"WELL DONE, THOU GOOD
AND FAITHFUL SERVANT!"

For this knight...with the help of his lady at his side...has guarded his heart!